AMERICAN SPORTS HEROES OF TODAY

Colorful profiles of forty of our greatest recent sports heroes in eleven different sports.

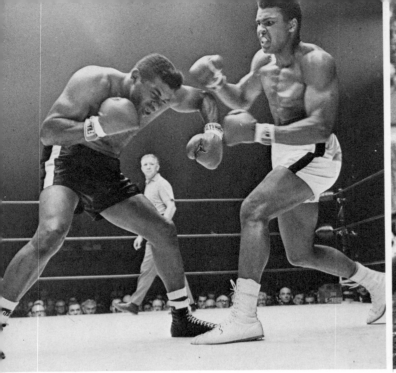

AMERICAN SPORTS

HEROES OF TODAY

by Fred Katz

Illustrated with photographs

RANDOM HOUSE · NEW YORK

Copyright © 1970 by Random House, Inc. All rights reserved under International and Pan-American Copyright Conventions. Published in the United States by Random House, Inc., New York, and simultaneously in Canada by Random House of Canada Limited, Toronto. Library of Congress Catalog Card Number: 70-117545. Manufactured in the United States of America. *Designed by Ted Burwell.*

For Elsa,
the one who stood out in the crowd

INTRODUCTION

For many years people thought that no era in athletics ever would surpass the Golden Twenties. That was the time of Babe Ruth, of Jack Dempsey, Red Grange, Bobby Jones, Bill Tilden and Johnny Weissmuller. These were towering figures, the greatest performers in the history of their respective sports.

And yet an era has come that does indeed challenge the Golden Twenties. It began in the 1960s and is continuing today. The new era has no flashy nickname, but catchy phrases are unimportant. What matters is that athletes in this era have done, and are doing, things once thought out of reach. The word "impossible" is taking on less and less meaning in sports.

Break Ruth's record of 60 home runs? Impossible! That's what everyone thought for years. But Roger Maris came along in 1961 and hit 61. Break Ty Cobb's record of 96 stolen bases? Impossible! But Maury Wills came along in 1962 and stole 104. One man score 100 points in a single pro basketball game? Impossible! But Wilt Chamberlain did it, also in 1962.

The "impossible" feats of the era roll on. Few people thought 22-year-old Cassius Clay could take the heavyweight championship away from Sonny Liston. But Clay did it, in 1964. The next year Sandy Koufax became the first man to pitch four no-hitters in a major-league career. In 1966 Frank Robinson became the first man to win baseball's Most Valuable Player award in both leagues. In 1967 young Jim Ryun became the fastest middle-distance runner in history, setting world records in both the mile and half-mile. Denny McLain was the hero of 1968, becoming the first pitcher to win 30 or more games in 34 years. Joe Namath turned pro football upside down when he led the Jets of the ten-year-old American Football League to a Super Bowl victory over Baltimore of the 50-year-old National Football League. And in the 1969 season Bobby Orr did things on ice that no one had ever done before and became the first defenseman to lead the National Hockey League in scoring.

Impossible! But true.

The era has been notable, too, for the many superb athletes who won over and over again—an "impossible" feat in itself considering the fantastic level of competition. Bill Russell became the greatest winner of all time, leading the Boston Celtics to the championship 11 times in 13 years. A. J. Foyt won the biggest of all auto races, the Indianapolis 500, three different times. Starting in 1958, Arnold Palmer won the most prestigious of all golf tournaments, the Masters, four different times, and Jack Nicklaus won it three other years. Lew Alcindor played in only two losing basketball games all through college. Roberto Clemente won four National League batting titles.

All of the athletes mentioned above have been included in this volume, plus many, many more. A few have retired. Others are nearing the end of long and distinguished careers. And still others may have even greater accomplishments ahead of them.

Each athlete in this book is an authentic American sports hero. Some also will become new legends in the world of sport, remembered by future generations as we remember the heroes of the Twenties. These great modern athletes have reached the pinnacle of success because they did away with the word "impossible"—and substituted the words "I can."

ACKNOWLEDGEMENTS

I am grateful to four other writers for their assistance in preparing this volume. They are John Devaney, a free-lance writer from New York City; Bill Libby, a free-lancer from Los Angeles; Lou Prato, News Editor of WWJ-TV in Detroit; and Nick Seitz, Features Editor of Golf Digest.

Devaney wrote the chapters on Hornung, Namath, Nicklaus, Unitas and Wills. Libby contributed the ones on Chamberlain, Clay, Koufax, Marichal and Palmer. From Prato came the pieces on Aaron, Clemente and Frank Robinson. Finally, I am indebted to Seitz for the stories on Maris and Mays.

It has been my pleasure to work with these four fine writers through the years at *Sport* Magazine, and the pleasure is mine once again. Many thanks to them all.

Fred Katz

CONTENTS

AMERICAN SPORTS HEROES OF TODAY

Henry Aaron shows the fierce determination and concentration that helped make him one of baseball's greatest hitters.

HENRY AARON

Henry Aaron trotted around third base. He could hear the cheers of the excited Atlanta Braves fans. Up ahead, he could see his happy teammates gathering around home plate to welcome him.

Henry had never been happier than he was at that moment. It was July 14, 1968, and he had just hit the 500th home run of his major league career. Two men crossed the plate in front of him and now every person in Atlanta Stadium was on his feet cheering for him.

When Aaron reached home plate he was mobbed. The 34,283 fans continued their loud standing ovation and the game with San Francisco came to a halt. Then, the President of the Braves, William Bartholomay, handed Henry a large trophy to mark the occasion and a smiling Aaron accepted with his usual graciousness.

A few minutes later, as Aaron ran out to his position in right field to start the fourth inning, the pitchers in the Braves' bullpen called him over to shake his hand. And again, the fans went wild. It was several minutes before the game could resume. When it did, the Braves went on to a 4–2 victory. Once more, Henry Aaron had powered the Braves to victory, this time with a memorable three-run homer.

Aaron had been leading the way for Braves victories for nearly two decades. He was already a star when the 1960s began, having won two league batting titles and a Most Valuable Player Award in the '50s. In the 1960s, Henry set the pattern for star consistency. In fact, he was so consistent that he was often taken for granted.

His 500th homer was a typical example. That homer made him the eighth greatest home run hitter in baseball history. But few fans realized Aaron had hit so many homers. And most fans had not realized that Henry was one of baseball's all-time leaders in total hits until he was honored in May of 1970 for hitting the 3,000th of his career. He thus became the first man ever to achieve both 3,000 hits and 500 home runs.

Surprisingly, Henry was not very big physically, at 6 feet, 180 pounds. His power at the plate came more from the snap of his amazingly strong wrists as the bat met the ball than from his size.

Although his accomplishments may have been neglected by some, he always has been appreciated by the Braves—first in Milwaukee and then Atlanta. He holds practically every all-time Braves hitting record. His .313 lifetime average at the end of the 1960s was the second best among the major league's active players.

Aaron's value was not all a matter of statistics. "More than anything, Henry is a game winner," says Paul Richards, the Atlanta General Manager. "He wins games with his head, with his legs and with his arm as well as his bat. I can't count the times he's thrown the tying or winning run out at the plate, or stolen a big base, or tripped somebody into making a foolish play. Henry does it all."

One reason Henry never achieved the recognition he deserved is his rather shy and retiring personality. He rarely complained or sounded off but this quiet attitude hid an active mind and a competitive spirit.

One day in 1955 when he was just starting out with the Braves, rain halted a game with the old New York Giants. Henry began playing checkers with a reserve catcher named Charlie White. White studied the board and deliberated a long time, then finally made his move. He looked at Henry who seemed sound asleep. "Wake up, Henry," White said sharply. "It's your move." "Oh," said Henry who immediately reached for a checker and made a triple jump!

Henry Aaron was born on February 5, 1934, in Mobile, Alabama. One of his younger brothers, Tommie, also plays for the Braves.

Henry didn't play much baseball as a youngster. He preferred to read instead.

Besides, his high school didn't have a baseball team. Later, he began hanging around the sandlots and soon began dreaming of playing professional ball. He was playing semi-pro ball at three dollars a game when the Indianapolis Clowns of the Negro American League saw him. This was at a time when few Negroes were playing in the majors and many great Negro stars played in the Negro leagues. For young players there was a chance of being picked up by a major league team if they performed well

Heading for first, Aaron watches the ball he has just hit to right field.

in the Negro Leagues. So, for $200 a month, Henry went to play for the Indianapolis Clowns.

He was soon spotted by the Braves, who were still playing in Boston. They signed him, then sent him to their minor league team in Eau Claire, Wisconsin. He played so well there in 1952 that they promoted him to Jacksonville of the Class A Sally League. At Jacksonville he met Ben Geraghty, who was the manager. Geraghty's fair and soothing treatment of young ballplayers left a lasting impression on Henry.

In one game Henry was a demon on the base paths. He got to first and stole second three times. But each time he moved off the base before the second baseman returned the ball to the pitcher. All three times he was tagged out.

"Ben really chewed me out for that," Henry recalls. "But he did it in such a way that I didn't feel so bad. He was the best manager I played for."

After one year of training under Geraghty, Aaron got a chance with the Braves. The Braves were now in Milwaukee, having left Boston the year before. But Aaron attracted little attention. Such big name players as Warren Spahn, Lew Burdette and Ed Mathews overshadowed him.

In spring training, Aaron got his first big break. The regular left fielder, Bobby Thomson, broke his ankle. Manager Charlie Grimm called Aaron aside.

"Kid, left field is yours," he said.

Recalling that moment years later, Aaron said, "I didn't know what to say. He gave me the big job and there were two other guys in front of me, players who had more experience. He showed a lot of confidence in me."

When Aaron went to bat for the first time, the rival catcher sneered. He noticed that Henry batted cross-handed and he mocked him: "Hey kid, you're holding the bat wrong. You ought to hold it so you can read the label."

Henry turned and looked directly at the catcher. "I didn't come here to read," he said. "I came here to hit." With that he drilled the next pitch to the outfield for his first base hit.

Henry had a fair season as a rookie but gave no indication of the brilliance ahead. On September 5, he was batting .280 with just 13 homers when he broke his right ankle sliding into third base during a game against Cincinnati. That put him out for the rest of the year.

The next season he showed the power that would hoist him to the top of his profession. He drove in 106 runs with 27 homers, 37 doubles and 9 triples while hitting .314. One year later he won his first batting crown with a .328 average.

Then came 1957. With Aaron powering the way, the Braves made a run for the pennant that had narrowly eluded them the previous four years. On September 23, Henry slammed a two-run homer in the last of the 11th inning, clinching the pennant and sending the Braves into the World Series.

Henry led the league in home runs with 44 and RBIs with 132. He also had an average of .322 and was voted the Most Valuable Player in the league. He continued his lusty hitting in the World Series, blasting Yankee pitching at a .393 clip with three homers and seven RBIs as the Braves won the World Championship.

Milwaukee repeated as the National League champ in 1958. Aaron hit only 30 home runs but raised his average to .326. The next year Henry won his second batting title with a .355 average and just missed the Triple Crown as he also drove in 123 runs and had 39 homers.

As the 1960s dawned, it appeared that

both Aaron and the Braves would continue to dominate the National League. Aaron did but his team didn't. The Braves finished second in 1960 but didn't finish that high again until 1969.

Meanwhile, Henry was working his way through opposing pitchers. Only twice did his average slip below .300. And he led the league three times in home runs. In two other years he hit 45 and 44 homers, but didn't win the home run crown. And each year he was named to the league All-Star team, making it for 15 consecutive years when the decade ended.

Early in his career, teammates tagged Aaron with the nickname "Hammering Henry" because of his ability to slug home runs. As 1970 began, Henry earned a real hammer. On April 13, he slammed the longest home run ever in Atlanta Stadium. By actual measure of a Georgia Tech engi-

neer, the ball travelled 503 feet, landing on seat 107, aisle 324, row 2 in the upper left field deck. Not only did the homer account for two runs in a 9–3 victory, but it also was the first time anyone had hit a homer to that spot in Atlanta Stadium. To mark the momentous blast, the Braves painted a large hammer at the spot where the ball hit.

Hammering Henry undoubtedly will get more home runs before he is through. And if he plays most of the 1970s, he could break one of the most treasured records in baseball —Babe Ruth's career homer mark of 714.

So, by the time he quits, Hank Aaron could be remembered as the greatest home run hitter of all time. But Henry has another way of looking at himself.

"I can't change my ways now," he says. "I play my own natural way. I know I'm not flashy; I don't try to be. I just want to be remembered as plain Henry Aaron."

Aaron waits in the on-deck circle during a game in 1969.

LEW ALCINDOR (Kareem Abdul-Jabbar)

The game promised to be a classic. The year was 1965 and the game featured two of the finest high school basketball teams in the country: Power Memorial from New York City and DeMatha Prep of Hyattsville, Maryland. Power brought a fantastic winning streak of 71 games to the contest. And DeMatha knew there was only one way to keep Power from making it 72. It had to stop Power's 7-foot-1 center Lew Alcindor. The year before, Alcindor had scored 35 points when Power defeated DeMatha 65–62. DeMatha put its two biggest men on Alcindor and slowed down the game. Surprisingly, the plan worked. Alcindor scored only 16 points and DeMatha won, 46–43.

The defeat was the first Alcindor had tasted since he was a high school freshman. He admitted years later that he had felt very sad about the loss, but said that he had gotten over it in a few hours. "Anybody can lose," he said. "The idea is to make losing a novelty, not a bad habit."

Almost all his life Lew Alcindor has been a winner. He has succeeded because he is bright, he works hard, and is marvelously coordinated. His most obvious advantage, though, is his size. Lew was already 22 inches long when he was born on April 16, 1947. And he grew to near-giant size although his father and mother were only moderately tall.

In sixth grade Lew was already six feet tall. One day in class a teacher asked him, "Lew, why aren't you sitting down?" Lew replied, "I am sitting down."

When he entered the eighth grade he was 6-foot-6. Near the end of the year he received a scholarship to Power Memorial, a private school with a tradition of good bas-

ketball teams. When Lew enrolled as a freshman he was 6–10. After growing so quickly, Lew was awkward and uncoordinated. In his freshman year Power lost five games and Lew averaged only 12 points a game. But the next season Power and Alcindor were off and running, beginning the winning streak that would finally be snapped at 71.

Even as a sophomore, Lew received attention from college scouts. Lew's coach, Jack Donohue, tried to protect him from the pressure as much as possible. He protected Lew from newsmen and handled the correspondence with colleges. When Lew was a senior Donohue was named coach at Holy Cross College. It was obvious that Holy Cross hoped Donohue would bring Lew with him. But that hope was disappointed. Out of courtesy to his coach, Lew made a visit to the college. But he soon narrowed his choice of a college down to the University of Michigan or the University of California at Los Angeles (UCLA). He finally chose UCLA because he was attracted to sunny California and because UCLA had shown its basketball power by winning two straight national championships.

At UCLA, Lew was officially proclaimed to be 7 feet, 1⅜ inches tall. He continued to be listed at that height even after he left UCLA, but many people believe he is actually taller. Some centers who have played against him believe he's closer to 7-foot-six.

Lew was devastating from his very first game at UCLA. He played with the freshman team against the UCLA varsity which was the defending national champion. The winner? The freshmen, 75–60. The freshmen won 21 straight that year and Lew averaged 33 points a game. "He could have

7

Alcindor celebrates UCLA's NCAA championship in 1967.

scored more if he was the hungry type," said UCLA coach John Wooden. "The best thing Donohue did was develop an unselfish attitude in the boy. Lew had the ability to be a star but Donohue taught him to be a member of the team."

After a year at UCLA Lew thought he had made a mistake in choosing the school. Lew had grown up in a black neighborhood in New York and was very conscious of the social condition of black people. He felt the people he met around UCLA were out of touch with black people. "They are not for real," he said. "They do not seem to know what's going on."

Lew's public remarks didn't make him very popular in Los Angeles, but UCLA basketball fans forgot about them once he took the floor. In his first game, against Southern California, Lew hit on 23 of 32 field goal attempts and on ten of 14 foul shots for a total of 56 points. It was the

most he would ever score in college, and it was almost as if he were saying, "Okay, I've proved I can score a lot of points. Now let's play basketball the way it was meant to be—as a team game." And he did. He set up plays, passed to the open man, and controlled the boards at both ends of the court. On defense he intimidated opponents even when he wasn't actually blocking their shots. Yet at the same time he was the second highest scorer in the country with an average of 29 points per game and his shooting average was an incredible .667.

Even the college rules-makers were concerned with Alcindor. At the end of his sophomore year they made "dunking" illegal. There was little doubt that the rule was aimed at Alcindor who, on occasion, had slammed the ball through the hoop with incredible force.

After the regular season UCLA went into the NCAA tournament. After winning easily in the early rounds they played Houston in the semi-finals and Lew faced Houston's Elvin Hayes, one of the few college men capable of challenging Lew. But Alcindor blocked three of Hayes' shots in the opening moments of the game and UCLA went on to a 73–58 victory. UCLA beat Dayton in the finals, 79–64, making them national collegiate champions.

After the tournament Elvin Hayes' battle cry was, "Wait'll we get 'em in the Dome!" UCLA and Houston were already scheduled to play in Houston's huge Astrodome in January 1968. When the game finally arrived, UCLA had a 47-game winning streak and Houston hadn't lost since its last meeting with UCLA. More than 52,000 came to see the game, the largest crowd in college basketball history. Millions more watched on national TV.

Unfortunately, the showdown was flawed a bit. Alcindor had suffered a scratched eyeball the week before and he still was having problems with his vision. Hayes dominated the game, scoring 39 points and Houston won 71–69. Lew hit on just four of 18 shots, and scored only 15 points.

Now it was Alcindor's turn to work for revenge. When the two teams met once again in the NCAA semi-finals, Houston had the winning streak—30 games. But Houston didn't stay unbeaten long. Behind Alcindor, UCLA crushed the Cougars, 101–69. The next night, UCLA had an easy time in the finals, beating North Carolina, 78–55.

Before his senior year, Alcindor had a chance to sign a possible million-dollar contract with the Harlem Globetrotters. But Lew was in college for the school work as well as the basketball. "A million dollars is a lot of money," he said. "But it's not enough to convince me to drop out of school . . . I want to grow a little bit inside. Then I'll be worth more."

Lew's final year at UCLA was nearly a copy of the others. In fact the Bruins made winning seem almost monotonous. Even Coach Wooden became weary of people taking UCLA's winning for granted. "I'll be glad when I can coach to win again instead of not to lose," he said at midseason.

Before the 1968-69 season was over UCLA did lose one game—to crosstown rival Southern Cal, 45–43. Except as a matter of pride, the loss meant little to Lew and UCLA, because they had clinched their conference title long ago.

In Alcindor's last NCAA tournament, UCLA got a scare in the semi-finals when underdog Drake pulled within one point with eight seconds to go. But UCLA won, and then romped over Purdue in the finals, 92–72. Alcindor ended his college career in typical fashion with 37 points and 20 rebounds. Usually emotionless on the court, he was stirred up for the Purdue game. "Wow," he said in the locker room later, "today after I came to the bench I was yelling. Wow, I was excited."

After the season Lew signed with the Milwaukee Bucks of the NBA for a $1.4 million guarantee. Although he also received

During the 1969 NCAA tournament Lou demonstrates his ball-handling skill. UCLA won its third championship in a row.

a huge offer from the New York Nets of the ABA, he wanted to play in the older league for more than money. The NBA was the league of Wilt Chamberlain, Willis Reed, Nate Thurmond, Wes Unseld, Elvin Hayes —the best centers in basketball. Lew wanted to go where the competition was, to prove himself against the best.

In his first pro game Lew scored 29 points, got 12 rebounds and blocked six shots. Lew was far from satisfied. "I made too many mistakes," he said. "I suddenly discovered there was more to basketball than we learned in high school and college."

One thing Lew set about doing was developing a hook shot. He hadn't needed it in college, because he towered over most of his opponents. But in the NBA he found that his turn-around jump shot could be blocked by a good opponent. Gradually Lew gained confidence in the hook and by the middle of the season it was his biggest offensive weapon.

In other areas of the game Lew's developing skills were just as startling. He could handle and dribble the ball as few big men ever had. He was also superb in getting the ball off the defensive boards and whipping it out to a guard to start the fast break.

By the end of the season Lew was second in the league in scoring, with a 28.8 average. He was third in rebounding average with 14.5 a game. He had led Milwaukee to a regular-season record of 56–26, second best in the entire league and a fantastic improvement over the team's 27 wins the year before.

In the first round of the 1970 playoffs, Milwaukee beat Philadelphia four games to one. But they were eliminated in the second round by a smoother, stronger New York team. In his ten playoff games Lew averaged 35.2 points.

No one had greater appreciation for Lew's performance than New York's center Willis Reed, the NBA's Most Valuable Player in 1969–70. "Nobody of his age has comparable talents," said Reed. "He has the ability, he has the speed and he's agile. Given time, he'll be the best center in the league."

In the NBA, Alcindor faced such great players as New York's Willis Reed.

LANCE ALWORTH

Practice was over and most of the San Diego Chargers were in the locker room. But the place-kickers were still on the field practicing and rookie Lance Alworth decided to join them. Alworth was a pass receiver, not a kicker, but he liked to be where the fun was and he couldn't resist trying to match kicks with the others.

Lance approached one of the footballs and brought his foot back. Just then a teammate playfully shoved Lance aside. A sharp pain shot through his right thigh. He limped back to the locker room, thinking he had pulled a muscle.

But as the 1962 season passed the pain in Lance's thigh got sharper. He couldn't run at full speed or make his moves as a receiver. He played only four of the Chargers' 14 games and caught only 10 passes. Worst of all, some of his coaches and teammates thought he was faking the injury. "There even were articles in the papers saying I was chicken," Alworth recalled years later.

After the 1962 season Lance had his leg examined in New York. There he was told that he had not just pulled a muscle, he had torn it. Lance underwent an operation to repair the damage. Then came the hardest part: he had to regain his speed, earn the respect of the Chargers, and win a starting position in the line-up.

During the off-season Lance did exercises, lifted weights, and ran mile after mile. Just before the '63 season, he ran 100 yards in less than ten seconds, not quite as fast as he had run in college, but fast enough. He became a regular, caught 61 passes in 1963, and made the All-AFL team.

If the Chargers still doubted Alworth's courage, all they had to do was watch Lance's dare-devil style of pass-catching.

Lance leaped like a deer, flying high in the air to get the ball. Soon his teammates started calling him "Bambi." Instead of wondering if he was a coward, they began to fear for his safety. "Someday someone's going to hit you while you're still in the air," they told him, "and your career will be over."

Lance Alworth makes an acrobatic leap for the ball as Johnny Robinson (42) and Fred Williamson of Kansas City close in on him.

11

But Lance would smile. "I feel I'm probably in a better position than people who have their feet on the ground," he'd say. "When I get hit, I'll just get pushed forward or turned end over. People who have their feet on the ground are going to get twisted."

Lance's best argument was his performance. Because of his combination of speed, timing and balance many experts soon considered him the finest receiver in either league. Between 1963 and 1968 he gained more than 1,000 yards in each of six straight seasons—a pro football record. In the last game of 1969 he added another amazing accomplishment. That game was the 96th in a row in which he had caught at least one pass. This broke the record of 95 games set 24 years earlier by the legendary Don Hutson.

At the end of the decade Lance was only 29 and had much of his career ahead of him. But he also knew that it would get harder each year. His age would begin to slow him down, but more important, he had become a marked man. Opponents were double- and triple-teaming him on his pass patterns. And he often took a fierce beating even before going out on his patterns; he would get knocked down at the line of scrimmage, pick himself up, and get hit again as he headed downfield. (Defensive players may make contact with a pass receiver until the pass is in the air.)

At 6-foot, 180 pounds, Lance was small for pro football, and opponents hoped they could wear him down. But they found out it took a lot to put Alworth on the sidelines. He has played at different times with broken ribs, with a broken wrist and with a broken bone in his hand. "I get hurt but I play," he said. "I always play."

Many pro athletes play mainly for the money, but for Alworth there were also other reasons. "I had a good, soft child-

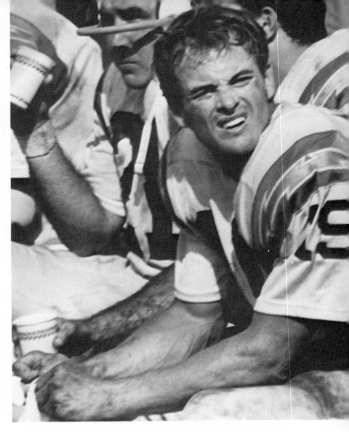

Alworth relaxes on the bench.

hood," he has said. "I didn't want for anything. But I've always loved football and taken pride in myself, and I've always forced myself to work hard enough to stay ahead of guys who were hungrier than I was. I didn't have to. I could've sat back and still been good. But not good enough."

Lance is the son of an oil executive and was born on August 3, 1940, in Houston, Texas. By the time he got to high school the family was living in Brookhaven, Mississippi, a town of 6,500. Lance excelled in all sports and won 15 letters. The New York Yankees thought he would make a fine major-league shortstop and offered him a $25,000 contract. Lance was tempted, but he liked football better and his father convinced him he should go on to college.

Soon after graduating from high school Lance married his childhood sweetheart, Betty Allen. Lance was 17, Betty 15. Lance was planning to attend the University of Mississippi. But when the university found out he was married, it hesitated about accepting him. Although Mississippi finally agreed to admit him, Lance decided he would be happier somewhere else.

He finally entered the University of Arkansas, and he never regretted his choice. In his three varsity seasons as a running back—1960–62—he led the Razorbacks to three straight 8–2 records. As a junior he was the top punt returner in the nation and in his senior year he gained 906 yards rushing. He was also a good student and made the Academic All-America teams all three years.

During his college career Lance didn't consider playing pro ball seriously. But when the San Francisco 49ers of the NFL made him their first draft choice and the Chargers of the AFL picked him in the second round, he changed his mind in a hurry. Both clubs thought he would be too small to be a pro running back, but thought he would make a great flanker.

The 49ers sent their head coach, Red Hickey, to see Lance at his home in Mississippi. When Lance asked for a contract guaranteeing that he would not be cut from the squad, Hickey refused. "In our league we just don't give no-cut contracts to rookies," he said. Hickey finally changed his mind and offered a no-cut contract. This time Lance refused and a short time later he signed with San Diego for a $10,000 bonus and a $15,000 contract.

Alworth joined the AFL in its third year when it was still struggling for recognition as a major league. Within a couple of seasons Lance was playing a big role in helping the AFL gain that recognition. Time after time he made impossible, leaping catches. In a game against Oakland in 1966, quarterback John Hadl threw a long desperation pass, which Alworth caught for a 43-yard gain. "I thought it would be intercepted,"

After outrunning his defenders, Alworth waits all alone for the ball.

New York Jet defenders grab desperately for Alworth as he heads for the goal.

said Charger coach Sid Gillman. "But there's only one Lance Alworth."

Any praise from Gillman was welcome, since he had often been Alworth's toughest critic. Gillman pressured Alworth to improve his moves instead of relying only on his speed and his good hands. And he insisted that Lance learn to block, like the rest of the Charger ends. Blocking wasn't easy for the frail-looking Alworth at first. "The only person I hurt was myself," he said. But he lifted weights, did isometrics and gradually made himself stronger. Soon he began to enjoy blocking. And he earned new praise from Gillman. "Lance could charm the money belt off Jack Benny," Gillman said, "but don't let him fool you. Deep down, he's a killer."

Off the field Alworth combined that charm and killer instinct to start a successful business empire. By 1969 he was close to being a millionaire, partly on his investments in fried chicken franchises. Coach Gillman, the Chargers and opponents all were quick to agree that that was the only "chicken" thing about him.

ARTHUR ASHE

Arthur Ashe gets set for a serve.

In 1968, Arthur Ashe had one of the greatest years an athlete has ever had. In August he won the United States Amateur Tennis Championship. Ashe was the first American to win the Amateur in 13 years and the first Negro male ever to win it. Two weeks later, he won the first U. S. Open, which included such professional stars as Rod Laver, Pancho Gonzales and Ken Rosewall. Finally, in December, Ashe helped lead the U. S. Davis Cup team to victory over Australia. It was only the second time in ten years that America had won the Cup.

Ashe, at the age of 25, was the new king of American tennis, and still an amateur. Directors of the professional tennis tour offered him $500,000 for a five-year contract if he would turn professional. He admitted he was tempted, but refused. Later he was offered $600,000 but again he said no.

Those who knew Arthur Ashe weren't too surprised. Ashe had always been fiercely independent. Becoming professional would mean that he had to play when he was told. As a black man in a game that was still closed to black men in some parts of the world, Arthur was deeply committed to the civil rights program and he wanted to have time available to participate in it too.

"I'm working with Whitney Young in the Urban League," Ashe explained. "One of our aims is to get jobs for dropouts, and we are meeting with success. I can do something no social worker can do. I can walk into any poolroom in Harlem, and those kids listen to me. I talk their language and they know who I am and what I've done. Each one of us who has a name has an obligation to the blacks that need help."

Arthur could remember when he was a young black growing up in Richmond, Virginia. He himself needed help, and he got it. It came from Dr. R. W. Johnson, a physician from Lynchburg, Virginia. Dr. Johnson first noticed Arthur at a Negro tennis club in Richmond. Arthur was ten years old and had been playing tennis for three years. Dr. Johnson was impressed by Arthur's ability and he invited Arthur to join the group he was coaching. Arthur accepted eagerly.

The first thing Dr. Johnson did was replace Arthur's old heavy racket with a newer, lighter one. During the next ten years Dr. Johnson helped pay for Arthur's equipment and fees. These were expenses that Arthur's father, a policeman, simply could not afford.

Ashe won his first national singles title in the Junior Indoor tournament in 1960, and repeated the next year. When he was 17 he went to St. Louis at the invitation of Richard Hudlin, a tennis official. He spent his senior year at Summer High School in St. Louis where he improved his game by facing the best young players in the country.

Then Arthur entered the University of California at Los Angeles. He chose the school for many reasons. For one thing, it was far from the racial discrimination of the South. He also liked the idea of playing tennis outdoors all year long. And Pancho Gonzales lived just a quarter mile from the UCLA campus.

"Skinwise, Gonzales was the nearest thing to me," said Arthur, referring to Pancho's Mexican ancestry. "And he was the greatest player in the world. That was a heck of a combination, a combination I couldn't resist."

Pancho and J. D. Morgan, the UCLA tennis coach, spent many hours helping Ashe with his game. One of Arthur's biggest problems was his large variety of strokes. "Ashe has about 16 different back-

hands," Pancho said at the time. "I wish he'd settle on a couple. He doesn't need that many."

Arthur also needed to concentrate more when he was in a match. Sometimes he'd forget all about his opponent and start thinking about a pretty girl he knew, or a movie he'd seen the night before.

Ashe managed to overcome these weaknesses and rose rapidly in the tennis ranks. In his senior year at UCLA he was rated second only to Dennis Ralston among American players. No Negro male had ever gone so high in tennis, but that in itself meant little to Ashe. "When I say I want to be the best, I don't mean the best Negro player," he said. "I mean the best player— period! I want to be Number One without an asterisk next to my name."

In late 1965 Ashe showed just how close he was to the top. He entered the Queensland Lawn Tennis Championship, a top-

Ashe sinks to his knees after missing an easy shot in the 1966 U.S. Championships.

Ashe darts to his left to return a backhand shot.

rated Australian meet which no American ever had won. Arthur beat both Fred Stolle and John Newcombe in straight sets to reach the finals. His opponent for the title was Roy Emerson, the No. 1 amateur in the world. Ashe had beaten Emerson a couple of months before, but few people thought he could do it again. But with the match tied at two sets apiece, Ashe broke Emerson's serve in the fifth set and won 6–1.

Arthur graduated from UCLA with a degree in business administration, then joined the Army as an officer for two years. Most of his tour was spent at the U. S. Military Academy, and he tried to play as much as his Army duties permitted. He wasn't at the top of his form in 1967, however, and lost both his Davis Cup matches to Ecuador in the American Zone final round.

But 1968 was a different story. He launched his winning season with a come-from-behind victory over Bob Lutz in the finals of the U. S. Championship. Then came the tournament everyone had been waiting for—the first U. S. Open. The Open was the first big American tournament in which pros and amateurs were permitted to compete against each other.

It turned out to be a bad ten days for the older and more experienced professionals. Ashe, who was not eligible for the large cash prizes, received only $15 a day for expenses. In his first three matches he defeated three pros and qualified for the final match against Tom Okker, a young Dutch pro. Arthur beat Okker three sets to two, wearing Okker down with his powerful serves and returns. Ashe won the title but Okker, who was the highest-finishing professional, received the $14,000 first prize.

In December of 1968, Ashe was the top-ranked singles player for the United States team in the Davis Cup match against Australia. He defeated Ray Ruffels, 6–8, 7–5, 6–3, 6–3, to start the U. S. on its way to its first Davis Cup victory since 1963. To Ashe, this team triumph meant more than any of his individual victories. "It's the big-

Ashe makes a strong backhand return to Bob Lutz in 1969 Davis Cup play.

gest thing in the world when you represent your country, not just yourself," he said. "If I were given the choice of winning a $20,000 tournament or playing on a winning Davis Cup team, where we get just living expenses, the choice would be easy: Davis Cup."

In 1969 Ashe turned professional, but on his own terms. He received no guaranteed income but he was free to play only in the tournaments he chose. He was confident he would earn as much as if he had signed a contract with a guarantee.

Ashe's first year as a professional proved to be both bitter and sweet. Tendonitis in his right elbow bothered him at times and he did poorly early in the summer. But by September he was close to his peak, again leading the U. S. to victory in the Davis Cup. It was the first time since 1949 that America had won two Cups in a row. Arthur won both his singles matches against Rumania in the Challenge Round. His second opponent, Ion Tiriac, was so demoralized by Ashe's strong serves that he walked off the court before the match was over.

Going into the 1970s, Ashe still had many goals in mind. There would be the Davis Cup each year. Arthur also badly wanted to win the British championship at Wimbledon. Perhaps he could accomplish the "Grand Slam"—win the U. S., French, Australian and British championships in one year. Only Don Budge and Rod Laver ever had done it.

Ashe also continued his work in civil rights. In early 1970 he tested South Africa's segregation policies by applying for a visa to compete there. He was refused a visa but called world attention to South Africa's discrimination. As long as there were civil rights battles to be fought, and tennis titles to be won, Arthur Ashe would be in there working at both.

JIMMY BROWN

When the 1963 season began, Jimmy Brown was on the spot. The year before, he had gained "only" 996 yards. Few running backs had ever gained so many yards but people had come to expect much more from Jimmy Brown, the greatest fullback in professional football's history. In seven years with the Cleveland Browns he had gained more than 1,000 yards in a season five times. When he fell to 996 yards some people whispered that Jimmy Brown was washed up.

Jimmy also was being blamed for getting Cleveland coach Paul Brown fired at the end of the 1962 season. There was a lack of communication between the players and the coach, and they felt that Paul Brown treated them more like robots than human beings. Jim Brown had spoken out as a representative of the team.

For a long time Jim had gone along with the coach. Even when he had called on Jim to carry the ball more and more each game, Jimmy never rebelled. In one game he carried 34 times. "Aren't those too many?" he was asked afterward. "Can't it shorten your career?"

"If the coach says carry 50 times," said Jim, "then I carry 50 times."

But in 1962 the Browns began to fall apart. Jimmy had severely injured his left wrist early in the season. It was painful for several weeks, forcing him to carry the ball in his right hand. This prevented him from using his right hand to push away tacklers and it cut down on his effectiveness as a runner.

When the coach began to suggest that perhaps Jimmy had lost his desire, Jimmy's patience ran out. Desire was one thing Jim Brown had never been without.

So Jimmy Brown spoke out against

Jimmy Brown

Coach Brown. Now he was forced to prove in the 1963 season that he had been right. Early in the 1963 season, under new head coach Blanton Collier, the proof seemed to be there. Jim had four strong games, and the Browns won them all. But the big test was the fifth game, against the Browns' bitter rival, the New York Giants.

The Giants scored first, on an intercepted pass, but the Browns charged back. They began a drive on their own 21-yard line, with Jimmy doing most of the ball-carrying. Jimmy ate up the yards, five or six at a time.

But he began to notice a strange thing. On practically every play he felt fingers poking through his face guard, trying to get at his eyes. After a while it began to take effect. "It seemed as though I was looking through a curtain," he said after the game. "Everything I saw was blurred."

But Jim wouldn't let the Giants know they were succeeding in impairing his vision. The way he continued to run, no one could have guessed. Jim finished that touchdown march by smashing over from the one-yard line to tie the score. But by halftime the Giants had taken a 17–14 lead.

Early in the third quarter, Jim Brown broke the game apart. He took a screen pass from quarterback Frank Ryan and zig-zagged 72 yards for a touchdown. A few minutes later he took a handoff on the Giants' 32. He glided easily toward his left. When his blockers had formed a wall and the Giant defenders had headed toward it, Jimmy cut across the grain to his right. It was an easy touchdown, his third of the game.

In the fourth quarter the Giants scored and came within four points, 28–24. Now Jimmy Brown demonstrated another of his talents—running out the clock. Starting on his own 20, he and teammate Ernie Green took turns carrying the ball. When they needed the first down, they got it. By the time they reached the goal line, only two and a half minutes were left. The game, in effect, was over.

"That's what did it," said Giants coach Allie Sherman afterward. "They controlled the ball. Put the headline on Jim Brown. It was one of his greatest days."

Despite the perfect start, the Browns lost four games in 1963, finishing second to the Giants in the Eastern Division. But that didn't take anything away from Jim Brown's personal accomplishments that season. He proved he was far from finished, setting an NFL rushing record of 1,863 yards. He had become the first running back ever to gain more than a mile in one season.

Jim Brown played two more years, leading the Browns into the NFL championship game both times. When he finally retired to pursue a movie career, he had set 11 NFL records. Among them were: most touchdowns for a career, 126; most yards rushing in a single game, 237; most seasons leading the league in rushing, 8; and best average per carry, 5.22 yards.

No running back ever had as well-balanced a blend of speed, power and grace as Jimmy Brown. At 6-foot-2, 228 pounds, he was built perfectly. He was small enough to be able to outrun most defenders, yet big and strong enough to break tackles. He preferred to ease his way out of a tough spot. A tackler would feel Jim's leg go limp and think Brown was falling to the ground. At just the right moment, Jim would jerk the leg away and be off again. But if Jim had to use his power, he could do that too.

"When he comes through that line, brother, you just have to forget about yourself and dive in there to try and stop him," said Giant linebacker Sam Huff, whose battles with Brown were classic. "You have to hit him from the knees down, or you don't have a prayer. Anything from the hips up, he'll either drag you with him or run right over you. He's run over me more than once."

Many people feel Jim Brown may have been the greatest all-round athlete who ever lived, even greater than Jim Thorpe. As a high school baseball player in Manhasset, New York, he attracted the attention of Casey Stengel, then with the Yankees. In basketball he averaged 38 points a game in his senior year. That same year in football he averaged 14.9 yards a carry.

All alone in the open field, Brown looks for the goal line.

(Big Mo) Modzelewski, "so I figured, 'Well, he's just another challenger.' "

The other Browns didn't make it any easier for Jim, hitting him harder than they normally would hit in practice. "But," said Big Mo, "he would bust out of their arms, and gradually you could see them gaining respect. The writing was on the wall for me, so I became his biggest rooter. You know, I doubt Jim ever knew the guys were hitting him extra hard."

Jim won the job as starting fullback and had one of his greatest days in the ninth game of his rookie season. Against the Los Angeles Rams, he scored four touchdowns and set an NFL record by gaining 237 yards rushing. He was to equal that record later on.

As the seasons rolled by, Brown began adding other records. But a certain frustration also grew, because the Browns couldn't seem to win a championship. Going into the 1964 season Cleveland had gotten into the title game only once during Jim's career and they had been crushed by Detroit, 59–14. Finally, in 1964, the Browns won another Eastern title and earned the right to meet Baltimore for the world championship.

The first half was a bruising, scoreless battle. On Jim's second carry he injured his hand and it began to swell up. On his third play he was kicked in the ribs. Several Cleveland players complained to the referees that Jimmy was being hit when he was down, but Brown himself said nothing.

Early in the second half Cleveland went ahead on a field goal. Then they quickly recovered a fumble. Jim's number was called. He took a pitchout, turned the left corner and went 46 yards, down to the Baltimore 18. On the next play Frank Ryan threw a touchdown pass to end Gary Collins. Two more Ryan-to-Collins TD plays were to follow, and Cleveland won, 27–0.

Going on to Syracuse University in 1953, he continued to play basketball and became an All-America in both football and lacrosse. Once, while warming up for a lacrosse game, he won the high jump at a track and field meet.

Shortly after college graduation he was offered $150,000 to become a heavyweight boxer. One prominent fight manager felt Jim had "all the basics to become the champ."

Jim turned the offer down to play football for the Browns, who had made him their first draft choice. During his first days in camp, it didn't look as though he had made the best choice. "He wasn't very sure of himself," said the Browns' veteran fullback, Ed

Brown hurdles over the line into the end zone against Baltimore.

Brown had not scored, but he had soft-ened up the Baltimore defense and had made it vulnerable to the pass. In all, Jim carried the ball 27 times for 114 yards. "If you weren't human," Frank Ryan told him in the jubilant locker room, "I would have given you the ball on every play."

Jimmy Brown played one more season, and came close to a second championship. But the Green Bay Packers beat Cleveland in the 1965 title game, 23–12. It wasn't one of Jim's better games, yet it didn't dim one bit of the luster of his career.

The following summer Brown announced his retirement. He wanted to devote full time to his movie career. Not surprisingly, he soon became a Hollywood star. He had proved long ago that when he set out to do something, he was bound to rise above the supporting cast.

DICK BUTKUS

When Dick Butkus was in the eighth grade he decided that someday he would be a pro football player. From then on he worked toward that goal. First he picked out the high school he wanted to play for—Chicago Vocational High School, which was much farther away from Dick's home than some other high schools. Dick chose Vocational because of its football coach, Bernie O'Brien, who was considered one of the finest coaches in all of Chicago. Dick reasoned, the better the coach, the better the player, and he was determined to be the best.

Early in the summer Dick traveled the five miles to Vocational High to introduce himself to Coach O'Brien. He told the coach he would be coming in September to play football. In the meantime, he said, he wanted a list of exercises to put him in top condition. The coach raised an eyebrow in surprise. He hadn't had a player quite that dedicated before. "I just want to get an early start," said Dick. "When September comes I want to be ready to go."

That fall Dick was ready, and he soon proved to be the hardest worker on the Vocational team. He was in love with football, and it was the only sport he allowed himself to play. "He didn't want to be distracted by anything else," Coach O'Brien recalled years later. "Every time you talked to him, all he wanted to talk about was football."

Dick also went to professional football games but he got restless just sitting and watching. "I have to be a player," he said. "I have to be closer to the action."

In his years at Vocational, Dick was usually in the middle of the action. As a senior he played both offense and defense. On offense he was a high school All-America full-

Dick Butkus

back. On defense, he made 70 percent of his team's tackles.

Dick's fierce desire and competitive spirit were caused partly by the kind of family and neighborhood he grew up in. He was born on December 9, 1942, and was one of nine children. He had four older brothers, the smallest of whom stood 6-foot-2 and weighed 200 pounds. Dick himself grew to

Butkus (51) zeroes in on Pittsburgh ball-carrier Charlie Bivins.

home, and because it was a member of the tough Big Ten conference. His brother Ron had also gone to Illinois and played football.

From Dick's first day of practice, Illinois coach Pete Elliott knew he would be one of the all-time greats. Butkus seemed to have an instinct for being at the right place at the right time to break up a play or tackle a ball-carrier. And his tackling was almost savage. In a game against Minnesota during his junior year he made 17 tackles and caused two fumbles with his hard hitting. This was a typical college performance for Butkus, except for one thing: in this game he was playing with the full use of only one arm because of a painfully inflamed left elbow.

That was only one of his fine performances during his junior year (1963). Against Ohio State he caught the Buckeye quarterback for a 12-yard loss on his first pass attempt. A short while later Butkus made a diving interception to set up Illinois' first touchdown. During the game, which ended in a 20–20 tie, he made or assisted on 23 tackles. Led by Butkus, Illinois won the Big Ten championship and defeated Washington in the Rose Bowl, 17–7. Dick was a unanimous choice for All-America.

Dick's performance was just as sensational during his senior year. He was voted college Lineman of the Year. His stature as a college player was confirmed in 1969 when a poll of coaches and football Hall of Fame members chose Butkus as one of only three players from the 1960s to be on the All-Time All-America team.

In the 1965 professional draft Dick was the first choice of the Chicago Bears of the NFL and the Denver Broncos of the AFL. Dick had always wanted to play for the Bears. He signed with Chicago for a reported guarantee of $200,000, a record at that time for a defensive player. "We gave

be 6-foot-3 and weighed 245 pounds, but for a long time, he says, "my brothers used to surround me like trees."

Dick's parents were immigrants from Lithuania (now part of the U.S.S.R.). They settled in a poor working-class neighborhood. Boys who grew up there became truck drivers, steel workers, policemen— and football players. "The well-off kid doesn't have the aggressiveness," Butkus has said, explaining his competitive spirit. "But the kid from the other side of the tracks, he's going to fight you down to the last straw."

When Dick graduated from high school in 1961, he was sought out by many major football colleges. He decided to go to the University of Illinois because it was close to

Butkus more money than we paid the entire team a few years ago," said George Halas, the Bears' owner-coach.

Butkus played one more game as a college star before joining the Bears—the 1965 College All-Star game. Several times Butkus brought down Cleveland's great fullback Jim Brown. In all, Dick made or assisted on 15 tackles. "Butkus is everything I've

Butkus attempts to knock down a pass while teammate Doug Buffone goes for the passer.

heard he is," Brown said later. "I'm glad the game is over."

In the Bears' first regular game of 1965, Butkus made 11 unassisted tackles against San Francisco. But he also was blocked out a few times by veteran 49er center Bruce Bosley. A few weeks later in a second game against the 49ers, Butkus wasn't stopped once by Bosley. "Every time I was supposed to block him," Bosley said, "he was going somewhere else. He sure improved fast."

Butkus impressed everyone in his first NFL season. In a game against Baltimore, which the Bears won, 13–0, Butkus caused one fumble and recovered two others. Colts coach Don Shula said afterward, "Butkus is so strong he can tackle the runner and search him for the ball at the same time." And Colts' guard Jim Parker called Butkus "the best rookie I've seen in my time in the league."

By the end of the season Dick had intercepted five passes to lead the entire Bears team. He would have been rookie of the year except that his teammate, running back Gale Sayers, had an equally great first season, setting a league record with 22 touchdowns. George Halas knew Butkus' value, though. He called Butkus the greatest lineman for the Bears in thirty years.

The late 1960s were painful years for the Bears. While Butkus continued to get better and better, the Bears seemed to get worse and worse. In 1969 they were woefully weak and won only one game. Somehow Butkus managed to stand tall above the ruins, and there was little doubt that he had become the finest middle linebacker in pro football. He had been invited to the Pro Bowl game every year—to no one's surprise. As George Halas had said, "I can't imagine a Pro Bowl game without Dick Butkus in it."

Neither could anyone else.

BILLY CASPER

Billy Casper, perhaps the best putter in golf, lines up a putt during the 1967 U.S. Open.

For 15-year-old Shirley Franklin, it was one of the biggest moments of her life. She was about to introduce her boyfriend, Billy Casper, to her parents.

As Billy stepped through the door of the Franklin residence, Mrs. Franklin gasped. Turning to her husband, she whispered, "Why, he's an old man!"

It's true that Billy was four years older than Shirley, but that wasn't the real problem. In a word, Billy was fat. He was less than six feet tall, yet he weighed well over 200 pounds. With his round face, and his stomach hanging loosely over his belt, he looked closer to 29 than 19.

Despite his appearance, Shirley agreed to marry him when she graduated from high school. As the years passed, Billy developed into a top professional golfer. But his excess weight still caused him embarrassing moments.

One of these moments occurred in 1959 when Billy had just won his first big championship, the U. S. Open. He was only 29, the youngest man to win the Open in 20 years. He was almost walking on air when he went up to the 18th green to claim his title. But a voice from the gallery quickly brought him back to earth.

"Here comes old jelly belly," said the heckler, and people couldn't help laughing.

That insult, and others like it, eventually sent Billy into action. In the early 1960s he consulted a Chicago physician about a diet. The doctor discovered that Casper was allergic to beef, pork and peas. Later, Billy also developed allergies to lamb, fowl, dairy food, wheat, beans and chocolate. That didn't seem to leave much for Billy to eat, but the doctor had the solution. He put Billy on a "wild game" diet. Soon Billy was eating moose, buffalo, elk, deer, quail, rabbit, bear and pheasant. He even tried hippo, yak and whale. Columnist Jim Murray wrote that Casper was the only golfer who had to send an Indian out to shoot his breakfast.

The diet was expensive, but it worked. Billy dropped from 228 pounds to 165. His playing weight stabilized at 185. Now the golf fans had a different reaction. In 1965, Billy overheard two of them arguing.

"I tell you, man, it's Casper," said one.

"Don't be ridiculous," said the other. "Casper is a fat guy!"

Billy decided to settle the argument. "If you're looking for Bill Casper," he told them, "I'm your man."

Billy's exotic diet brought him attention for a while, and there were no more insults about his weight. But one problem remained. Casper wasn't a colorful golfer and couldn't muster the fan appeal of golf's big three—Palmer, Nicklaus and Player. Billy played a quietly consistent game, but often newspapermen and golf fans focused their attention on the more dramatic leaders.

In the '60s Casper was golf's most consistently great performer. He almost never went into a slump and he finished near the top in almost every tournament. In 1968 a computer fed with information on the top 100 golfers on the professional tour showed that Casper had the lowest average score, the fewest bogeys and the fewest putts per hole.

Casper's style was unspectacular. He played a mental, not a physical, game. He didn't whack his drives a mile down the fairway, but he did position them with more skill than any golfer since Ben Hogan. Once he was on the green, he displayed as steady a putting touch as had ever been seen. He once accepted a challenge and sank 93 three-foot putts in a row.

Billy had one thing that made up for the lack of attention from the fans: money. Almost every year during the '60s he was among the top five money-winners. In 1968 he was the first, winning $205,168. He was only the second golfer in history to win $200,000 in one year.

Billy Casper was born on June 24, 1931, in San Diego, California. His father, an amateur golfer who played in the high 70s, started giving Billy lessons as soon as he was big enough to swing a club. Billy was such an eager pupil that he would practice his putting at night while a friend held a flashlight so that Billy could see the hole.

Billy was captain of his high school team at 15, and later won the San Diego County amateur and open championships. He accepted a golf scholarship to Notre Dame but stayed only one semester. Soon afterward he enlisted in the Navy where he was assigned to special services and continued to play golf regularly.

Once Casper became a professional in 1955, financial success came quickly. Traveling from tournament to tournament with his wife Shirley and their infant daughter Linda, he earned $18,700 in his second year—12th best on the circuit. The next year he won over $40,000. His fast start absolutely amazed some of the older veterans.

"He's Houdini!" said '56 PGA champion Doug Ford. "And he's a fighter. He expects every shot to go well for him, and that's the kind of attitude you need in this game. He's a winner."

Billy saved his greatest magic for the 1959 Open at the Winged Foot Golf Course in Mamaroneck, New York. In spite of a windstorm on the final day of play he beat Bob Rosburg by one stroke. Incredibly, he putted only 114 times in the 72 holes averaging only 1.6 putts per hole.

In 1960 he won the Vardon Trophy for

Casper connects with an iron shot from the edge of the fairway.

lowest average round on the tour, averaging 69.9. He won it again in '63, even though there was a time during the season when he thought his career might be over. Early that year he dislocated a bone and tore some muscles in his hand. He kept playing, but finally had to withdraw from the Tournament of Champions in Las Vegas during the last round, even though he was in contention for the title.

"That was the low point of my career," he has said. "For a while, I wondered if I'd ever play again. I visited several doctors without getting help. But finally an orthopedic man re-located a bone in my hand and I began to feel better almost immediately."

In each of the next two years Casper won four tournaments. But he was beginning to get the reputation as a golfer who won only the secondary tournaments and not the most important ones.

Casper put that charge to rest in the 1966 U. S. Open at the Olympic Club in San Francisco. Going into the last nine holes of the final round, Casper trailed Arnold Palmer by seven strokes. But Casper shot an amazing 32 on the last nine, Palmer shot 39 and they tied for the championship. In an 18-hole playoff the next day, Casper was behind after the front nine, by two strokes. But he overtook Palmer again, winning by four strokes with a 69. Billy Casper had won his second U. S. Open.

In 1968 Casper received all but one of the 38 ballots from the Golf Writers Association of America as the Golfer of the

On the last hole of the 1970 U.S. Masters tournament, Casper misses the putt that would have won the tournament. Casper tied with Gene Littler and won the Masters in a playoff.

Year. And in 1969 he was still going strong. When he won the $100,000 Bob Hope Desert Classic in February, it was his 42nd PGA Tournament victory. In early 1970 he added another major title when he won the Masters Tournament in Augusta, Georgia.

Off the golf course Billy kept busy, too. A devout Mormon, he traveled all over the world as a missionary for the Church. He also went to Vietnam at his own request. There he visited 45 Marine and Special Forces camps, showing films and giving golf tips.

It seemed likely that Casper might one day win the recognition of the fans—he had won nearly everything else.

WILT CHAMBERLAIN

In March of 1962, Wilt Chamberlain was nearing the end of his second season in the NBA with the Philadelphia Warriors. The Warriors were playing the New York Knicks a regular-season game in a small arena at Hershey, Pennsylvania. Chamberlain, the most devastating scorer basketball has ever known, was at his best.

He whirled right and left around the Knick centers Darrall Imhoff and Phil Jor-don to slam the ball down through the hoop with awesome force. He jumped, and banked in shot after shot while falling away from the basket. His teammates kept feeding him and he kept shooting and hitting. The Knicks fouled him and he stepped to the free-throw line to sink shot after shot.

The score mounted. The small crowd was amazed, roaring as Chamberlain headed for a record that few people dreamed was within

Wilt Chamberlain shows the great reach that has made him a basketball legend.

reach of a single player. The seven-foot, one-inch, 275-pound giant dominated this game as no man had ever dominated before. In this single game, Chamberlain tried more field goals, 63, and sank more, 36, than any player in pro basketball history. He tried 32 free throws and sank more, 28, than any pro player in a game before. He scored 31 points in one quarter and 59 in one half. Most amazing, he scored an even 100 points in the game.

When he sank his last basket, and his 100th point, the crowd stood and cheered him as few players have ever been cheered. The Warriors won, 169–147, and Wilt, as he ran off the court grinning, was proud to have done what perhaps no other player could do.

Although Wilt "The Stilt" Chamberlain has rewritten many pages of the basketball record book, he has not always been cheered and he has not always been able to grin contentedly and proudly. He has been one of the most controversial players in the sport's history. "I am a Goliath," he sighs. "And the world is made up of Davids. No one loves Goliath."

Wilt Chamberlain was born August 21, 1936, in Philadelphia. His father, who was a handyman, and his mother, who was a maid, raised eight children on less than $100 a week. Wilt grew so tall so fast, he was naturally attracted to basketball, especially in Philadelphia where basketball is a passion. At first, he was awkward and shy, but he learned fast against tough competition on outdoor courts. He often had the chance to play top college and pro players in pick-up games.

At Overbrook High School, he averaged 37 points a game, twice scored 90 or more in a game, and led his team to two city championships. He was already nearly seven feet tall and weighed 225 pounds. More than 200 colleges offered him basketball scholarships when he was a senior. He surprised everyone by selecting the University of Kansas. He said he wanted to attend a school away from home and liked Kansas' veteran coach, Forrest "Phog" Allen. It was suggested that Kansas had made unusual financial offers to Wilt to get him to come. Wilt denied these charges but they plagued him throughout his college career.

He was not happy with Kansas or with college basketball. Permitted by college rules to use zone defenses, opponents collapsed two or three men around him and roughed him up heavily. In his sophomore year Kansas lost the NCAA championship finals to North Carolina in three overtime periods by one point. Wilt's disappointment was heightened when the aging Allen was forced to retire before Wilt's junior year. A younger coach, Dick Harp, took over and the team faltered.

After two varsity seasons during which he averaged 30 points a game and Kansas won 42 of its 50 games, Wilt quit college and toured for a year with the Harlem Globetrotters. He enjoyed the clowning and traveling and called it "the greatest year" of his life, but then in 1959 turned to the NBA in search of greater challenges, prestige and financial rewards.

Philadelphia Warriors' owner Eddie Gottlieb gained the rights to Wilt, and signed him for $65,000 a season. Chamberlain averaged 38 points a game and was acclaimed Rookie of the Year and Most Valuable Player at the end of his first season. The Warriors finished second in the Eastern Division and lost in six games to Boston, the eventual league champion, in the divisional final playoffs.

In the following seasons Wilt continued to excel. In one 1960–61 game he collected 55 rebounds against the Celtics. The next year he averaged more than 50 points per game—still an NBA record—and during one streak he scored 50 or more in 45 consecutive games.

But Philadelphia continued its pattern of second-place finishes during the regular season and losses to the Celtics in the NBA playoffs. Wilt was bitterly criticized in Philadelphia as a selfish player who would not cooperate with his coaches, who scored his points but lost games, and who could not come through under pressure. He was often booed, even by home fans.

In 1962 the Philadelphia franchise was shifted to San Francisco and Wilt went with it. He averaged 44 points a game, but his transplanted team lost more games than it won, finished fourth and failed even to make the playoffs. In the 1963–64 season, Wilt began to shoot less and pass off more, averaged 36 points a game and helped his team bounce all the way to the Western pennant. The new Warriors won the divisional playoffs in a seven-game struggle with St. Louis, but lost four out of five in the finals against Boston.

When San Francisco faltered badly through the first half of the next campaign, Chamberlain was sold to the new club back in Philadelphia named the 76ers. That a club would even sell such a star cheapened Wilt's reputation, but San Francisco had been losing with him and was no longer eager to pay his salary, which had passed $100,000 a season.

With Wilt, the 76ers finished in third place at 40–40 and won a place in the playoffs. Again his team fought through six games with Boston in the playoffs, but lost the seventh, 110–109.

This Philadelphia team, however, was building around Chamberlain one of the great all-around clubs of all time. Rebounding, blocking shots, passing as often as he shot, Wilt's average fell to 24 points a game

in 1965–66 but he was named MVP and led his team to a splendid 55–25 record, one game ahead of Boston in regular season play. Then they promptly were blasted out of the playoffs by the Celtics again, this time in five games.

Finally, in the 1966–67 season, Chamberlain and the Warriors hit the top. They put together the greatest season in NBA history, 68–13, for another pennant. Chamberlain averaged 24 points and again gained the MVP honor.

Then came his finest moment. In the playoffs the 76ers beat Boston four out of five games, slaughtering them 140–116 in the last game. In the finals the 76ers beat Wilt's old team, San Francisco, in six games for the championship. "This is my first national championship. I've waited all my life for this," a weary, sweaty and wistful Wilt said in the tumultuous dressing room after the last game.

In the 1967–68 season, Wilt averaged 20 points a game, despite his worst-ever free-throw shooting percentage, .380. He set another record by making 702 assists—the most ever by a center in one season. Wilt was voted MVP for the third straight year and Philadelphia finished first for the third straight year. But Boston beat them again in the playoffs, in seven games.

After 10 years as a pro, Chamberlain had established enormous records, but he was still considered a troublemaker and a loser who could not get along with coaches and teammates. Admittedly a loner who demanded a high price for his services, Wilt asked the 76ers to be traded to Los Angeles, whose owner, Jack Kent Cooke, was willing to pay Wilt the $200,000 yearly salary he asked. Wilt hoped to make Southern California his permanent home.

In Los Angeles in the last season of the 1960s, Wilt joined super-stars Jerry West

Chamberlain and Boston's Bill Russell fight for a rebound during the 1965 NBA playoffs.

and Elgin Baylor in the most star-studded team ever assembled. But the Lakers were aging and injury-prone and it took some time to fit to each other's styles. In the end, the results were similar to the pattern Chamberlain's other clubs had established. The Lakers won the pennant with their best-ever record, 55–27, but lost to Boston in the seventh game of the playoffs, 108–106.

As the decade ended, Wilt Chamberlain held most of the NBA's major records. In 11 seasons, he had totalled more points, more than 27,000, and averaged more per game, 34, than any player in history. He had 15

Chamberlain pulls down rebound for the Lakers.

barely 50 percent of his free throws. And he was still considered a loser, whose teams had lost seven times in the playoffs to Boston and won only once. By contrast, Bill Russell had led Boston to 11 playoff crowns in 13 seasons.

A proud man, a wealthy bachelor who dressed in the finest clothes, drove the most expensive sports cars and lived in a lavish home in an exclusive section of Southern California, the great, bearded giant Chamberlain deeply resented his stature being so diminished. "Game after game, I played the pants off Russell, but my teams often lost to his only because my teams were not as good as his," Chamberlain complained.

"When my team was better, we beat his team out of three straight pennants. I always did everything Russell did, and scored, too, which he did not. They say I was selfish, but he played all his career for one team one way, while I played for different teams and changed my style to suit my teams."

In the first season of the new decade, the 1969-70 campaign, Russell had retired and without him Boston did not even make the playoffs. Chamberlain tore tendons in one knee late in 1969 and without him the Lakers sagged into second place. Still, Chamberlain made a remarkable recovery, returning at season's end to lead his team into the playoff finals. This time they lost to New York in seven games.

His gallant comeback earned him the kind of praise he had seldom enjoyed before. The fans in L.A. cheered Goliath as he had never known fans to do. Teammate Jerry West said, "We've all gained enormous respect for him." Said Wilt, "I always loved the game, even if it didn't always love me. I know now how easily this can end for me, like snapping a stick, and I am hoping some of my greatest accomplishments are yet ahead of me."

of the 16 highest-scoring games in history. He had collected 19,000 rebounds, second only to Boston's Bill Russell, and averaged 24 a game. He and Russell were the only centers among the all-time top 10 in assists.

Yet, he still was considered a freak, who made it on size, not skill. He had made

CASSIUS CLAY (Muhammad Ali)

In his last three fights, Sonny Liston had scored three one-round knockouts. In the last two he had won and then defended the heavyweight championship. Now, as he faced Cassius Clay in Miami Beach in 1964 with his famous, fierce scowl, he was a heavy favorite.

Clay, tall, handsome and boyish, barely 22 years old, had made fun of Liston but seemed no match for him in the ring. He'd had only 21 professional fights. He was fast and fancy, but did not seem strong. He bragged so much and composed such odd rhymes that he was regarded with good-natured contempt. "That big, bad, ugly bear I hate . . . Has got to fall within eight," he had said, but no one believed him.

The press had ridiculed him. The small crowd of 8,297 fans in Miami and 600,000 more in theaters across the country expected a slaughter. Most of them wanted to see the cocky Cassius get his comeuppance.

It was not to be. Dancing around swiftly, and jabbing sharply, Clay eluded Liston during the early rounds, making him seem clumsy. At the same time, Clay's attacks were successful—he cut Liston's face badly. But between the fourth and fifth rounds Clay's face suddenly contorted in pain. He rubbed furiously at his eyes with his gloved hands and he pleaded with his trainer, Angelo Dundee, to stop the fight. Something had gotten into Clay's eyes and he was nearly blind. Dundee tried to wash the substance out of Clay's eyes and urged him to carry on. Clay did, boxing desperately.

It was never determined what happened to Clay's eyes. He took a beating in the

Cassius Clay, who had recently changed his name to Muhammad Ali, scolds Sonny Liston before their second fight in Lewiston, Maine. He knocked Liston out in the first round.

fifth round, but just when referee Barney Felix was considering stopping the bout, Cassius' vision began to clear. In the sixth, Clay drove his fists into Liston. When the ball rang for the seventh round, Liston was sitting in his corner complaining of an injured shoulder. He refused to come out. Suddenly the fight was over. Clay leaped in the air, arms outspread, and then pranced around shouting, "I'm the greatest, I'm the king," as the fans watched, amazed and excited.

Before he left the ring, the new heavyweight champion of the world leaned over to the writers at ringside and contemptuously asked, "Whattaya say now?" Confronted by the press in his dressing room, he asked "Who's the greatest?" and insisted they answer, like the mirror on the wall, "You, king, are the greatest of them all," before he would answer their questions.

It was a wild moment in the brief, bewildering career of the most controversial athletic champion of the 1960s. In the course of his career he chose a new name, took membership in the controversial Black Muslim movement and was finally forced to give up his heavyweight crown.

Cassius Marcellus Clay, Jr., was born in Louisville, Ky., on January 17, 1942. His family was poor. Once when he asked his father why they weren't rich, the old man smiled wistfully and pointed to his son's brown skin. Cassius dreamed of having rich and beautiful things. Although his father was too poor to give him many things, he bought Cassius an expensive new bicycle when he was 12. Cassius rode it proudly to a carnival, and he parked it outside. When he returned, it was gone. A policeman, Joe Martin, found Cassius weeping bitterly, promising, "When I catch who stole it, I'm gonna whup him bad."

Martin suggested that if the youngster was going to fight, he should learn how. He took him to the Columbia Gym and introduced him to a boxing program. Cassius found he loved boxing, and he learned quickly. He never recovered his bike but he turned his attention to more expensive transportation. He used to walk to and from the gym past a Cadillac showroom. He assured the amused salesman, "Some day I'm going to be heavyweight champion of the world and rich and I'm gonna buy me the biggest and prettiest car you have."

Cassius was a poor student who barely graduated from high school, but he was a determined and hard-working student of boxing. He used to run to school rather than ride the school bus to build up his speed. And he would dodge rocks tossed at him by his brother to build his reflexes. One time he did get into trouble—he hit a teacher with a snowball. When he was called before a disciplinary board, he said, "I'm sorry. But I'm going to be heavyweight champion of the world."

Clay soon began winning as a boxer. At 18, he won National AAU and Golden Gloves titles and a place for himself on the 1960 U. S. Olympic boxing team, but he had to be talked into going to Rome to participate because he feared flying.

In Rome Cassius clowned around in the ring, often dropping his hands to his sides to taunt his foes. The swift Kentuckian defeated all his opponents and dazzled spectators. He won the gold medal in the light-heavyweight division. When a Russian reporter pressed him for his criticisms of America, Clay said, "Russian, we got qualified men working on our problems. We got the biggest and the prettiest cars. We got all the food we can eat. America is the greatest country in the world." In later years he was more critical of his country.

Returning to the United States, Clay was

hailed as a hero. He began to recite boastful little rhymes. One went, "They say the greatest was Sugar Ray . . . But they have yet to see Cassius Clay." Sugar Ray Robinson, the former welterweight and middleweight champion, who was known as the classiest boxer in history and was famous for living in grand style, was Clay's idol. Cassius vowed to surpass him. He bought elegant clothes, took out pretty girls and squirmed when passers-by did not recognize him. "Some day, everyone gonna know me," he vowed.

Clay received a $10,000 bonus for signing a contract with a syndicate of 11 wealthy businessmen who would manage his career and share in his winnings. The veteran Angelo Dundee became his manager. With his bonus, Clay was able to carry out his boast to the car dealer. He walked in and bought an expensive model.

Rapidly growing into a 6-foot-3, 210-pound heavyweight, he fought his first pro bout in October of 1960 in Louisville and won the decision. He knocked out his next five foes. He moved up the boxing ladder swiftly. In his 17th fight, in November of 1962, he knocked out Archie Moore, the light-heavyweight champion, in four rounds. Now, he boasted, he was ready for a heavyweight title shot.

Cassius traveled from fight to fight in a brightly colored bus. On the sides were painted, "Cassius Clay, the World's Most Colorful Fighter." He bragged to writers, "I am not only the greatest, but the prettiest. I'm as pretty as a girl because none of these other so-called fighters can even lay a glove on me."

He wanted to be best in everything. Once while eating dinner with an interviewer, he said, "Be sure and write in there that I chew and eat twice as fast as the average man." Soon Clay was even predicting the rounds in which he would stop his foes: "He knocks them out in the round he'll call . . . And that's why he's called the greatest of them all."

Sometimes his predictions came true, but skeptical sportswriters and fans remained unconvinced that Clay was a great fighter. In March of 1963, Cassius had a tough fight with Doug Jones in Madison Square Garden, New York. Most writers thought Jones deserved the decision. When it was announced that both judges and the referee awarded the fight to Clay, the outraged fans booed and threw trash into the ring. The reporters called the verdict a farce. Clay's next stop was London, where he stopped former British champion Henry Cooper in five rounds.

In February of the following year, Clay scored his astonishing upset of Liston. Fifteen months later, after other cities had refused to host a rematch, they met again in Lewiston, Maine. Again Liston was heavily favored, but he was knocked out in the first round by what most observers felt was a weak punch.

By the time he fought Liston the second time, Clay had announced he had joined the Black Muslim movement, an organization which practiced a form of Islam and advocated black separatism and self-help. It was accused of approving of violence and was feared by many whites. In conformity with his new religion, Clay announced that he had changed his name to Muhammad Ali.

Ali gave up his wealthy backers but kept Dundee as his manager. He began to associate mainly with members of the Black Muslims. He married, but later was divorced because he felt his wife was unsympathetic to his new beliefs. His association with the Muslims and his continuing boastfulness made him increasingly unpopular among whites and among some blacks.

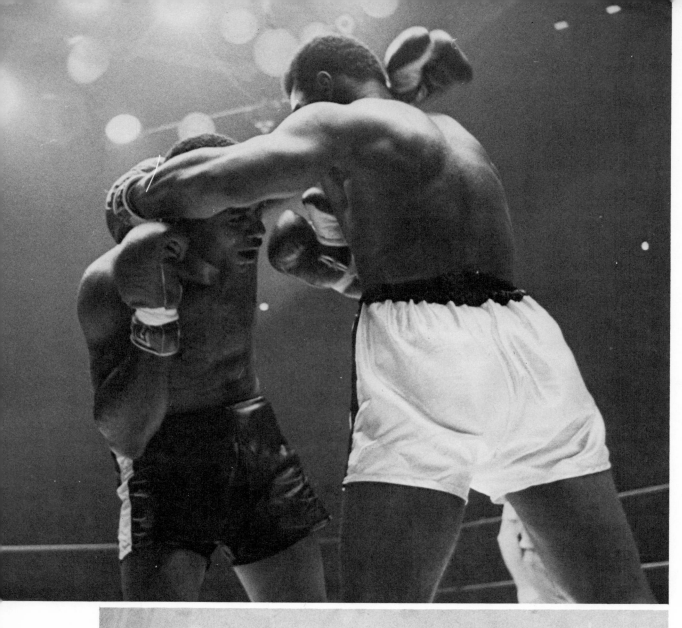

In November of 1965, Ali fought ex-champion Floyd Patterson. He completely dominated the fight, taunting Patterson and preferring to punish him rather than knock him out. He even protested when the referee stopped the fight in the 12th round.

In 1966, Ali defended his title five times. He decisioned George Chuvalo in Toronto, knocked out Henry Cooper and Brian London in England, knocked out Karl Mildenberger in Germany and Cleveland Williams in Houston. In 1967, Ali decisioned Ernie Terrell in Houston and stopped Zora Folley in New York. As it turned out, his fight with Folley was his last in the 1960s.

Ali refused to be drafted into the military service. In May of 1967, he was indicted by a federal grand jury. Ali contended he was a minister in his faith and so exempt, but the court convicted him, making him liable to a term of five years in jail. As the decade ended, he remained free while his case was appealed to higher courts. But he was repeatedly denied permission by various states to box again. Gradually he lost recognition as heavyweight champion. Jimmy Ellis, his former sparring partner, won a tournament to crown a new heavyweight champion, then lost the title to Joe Frazier. "Frazier's the champ now. I don't expect ever to fight again," Ali said sadly. "If they tell me to go to jail, I will go."

Ali's personality seemed to change with his fortunes. He said, "Maybe I'll go into show business. I'm the world's greatest actor." One brief attempt in 1969 was a failure, but he continued to appear on late-night TV shows. He still bragged, but in a subdued way. He suggested that his earlier antics had been stunts to gain publicity and draw big crowds.

Although his career was cut short, Ali had earned more money than any fighter in history—more than $5½ million. By the end of the decade much of it had disappeared, perhaps to the Muslim cause. Still, he had a fancy apartment in Philadelphia and lived a good, if quiet life. He had remarried and had a family to care for. He remained faithful to Islamic principals of cleanliness and virtue.

When he first began to fight in Louisville, the Kentucky lad once said, "Someday, I'm gonna drive down Walnut Street on Derby Day and all the people will point and say there goes Cassius Clay. Pretty girls will be there and I'll smell the flowers and feel the nice warm night air. Oh, I'm cool then, man, I'm cool. The girls are looking at me and I'm looking away."

His day of glory had come and swiftly gone. He had become Muhammad Ali, recognized wherever he went, but a lonely, haunted figure, who no longer chased girls, who was no longer permitted to box. Many people had changed their minds about him and now considered him unfortunate and unfairly treated. But others thought him foolish or even dangerous—to them he was a draft-dodger who had renounced his right to be champion.

When Ali had unwillingly retired he was undefeated in 29 bouts. With the passage of time, his reputation somehow had improved. Denied the chance to see him in action, observers were wondering if perhaps he really was what he had always claimed to be—the greatest.

Ali fights ex-champion Floyd Patterson (above) in November 1965. Ali won on a technical knockout in the 12th round. In his last fight of the '60s (below) Ali stands over Zora Folley in the fourth round. Folley got up but was knocked out in the seventh.

ROBERTO CLEMENTE

Roberto Clemente waits in the dugout for a game to start with the Giants.

Rain fell lightly on the streets outside the Cincinnati hotel and Roberto Clemente wondered if he would play baseball that night. He stood by the window of his room, feeling drowsy from lack of sleep. His back ached more than it had in days and his body felt tight all over.

Clemente turned and went back to lie down on the bed. He was tired, very tired. He tried sleeping for several hours but only tossed and turned. All the time he could feel the ache in his back, the pain in his arm, the sore muscle in his leg.

It was May 15, 1967, and a typical afternoon away from home for Roberto Clemente, star outfielder for the Pittsburgh Pirates.

Finally, it was time to go to the ball park. Roberto dressed slowly, trying to shake off the soreness he felt. Then he joined his teammates for the bus ride to Crosley Field.

Within hours, the game had started. The rain was still falling lightly when Clemente stepped to the plate in the first inning. He hadn't been able to relax since playing the night before and he still felt some aches through his body. But now he had to forget all that and bat against Cincinnati.

The Pirate shortstop, Maury Wills, was on first base. The Reds' pitcher, Milt Pappas, threw. Roberto swung and the ball sailed into the seats in right field. Pittsburgh led, 2–0, and Clemente was off to the most fantastic batting spree of his illustrious career.

In the fifth inning, Clemente hit another two-run homer off Pappas, making the score 4–0. When the Reds came back with three runs in the sixth, Clemente increased the Pirates' lead again in the seventh with a two-run double.

The Reds scored two more in their half of the seventh. So, the next time up in the ninth Roberto homered again. Then, as the Reds rallied in the last of the ninth, Clemente leaped high in the air at the fence to stop a probable Cincinnati home run. The Reds tied the score and the game went into extra innings.

Unfortunately, Roberto didn't come to bat in the tenth. The Reds won 8–7 and turned Clemente's momentous day into one of sadness.

"Yes, that was my biggest game," he recalled, "but not my best game. My best game is when I drive in the winning run. I don't count this one. We lost."

Clemente had never hit three home runs in one game before. Nor had he knocked in seven runs in one game either. But it was typical that in spite of Clemente's individual performance, the Pirates lost. That was Roberto's misfortune in baseball—playing with a loser.

Throughout the 1960s Clemente often complained that he was not receiving the recognition he deserved. And he was right. No matter what he did, it seemed his feats were always overshadowed by the poor play of the Pirates. In Clemente's 15 years with Pittsburgh, the Pirates won just one pennant and finished second once. They wound up in the second division nine times, six times since 1961.

Meanwhile, over the same period Roberto achieved one of the greatest individual records in the history of baseball. As the 1970s began, the Puerto Rican native had the highest lifetime batting average among active players—.314. Four times he had been the National League's batting champion. Only Hall of Fame stars Stan Musial, Rogers Hornsby and Honus Wagner had ever won more National League batting titles. Clemente's .357 average in 1967 was the highest in the National League since 1948.

But Clemente was not simply a super hitter. He was also one of the game's greatest defensive outfielders and would have been a major league All-Star on his fielding alone. He has literally run into walls to catch fly balls. Once in 1960 he broke his jaw while doing so. Roberto's muscular throwing arm is the most powerfully accurate one in the majors and Clemente says he learned to

Clemente, winner of four National League batting titles in the '60s, looks for another hit.

throw so well by tossing around the javelin as a youngster in Puerto Rico.

Although he now lives in the city of San Juan, Clemente was born on August 18, 1934, in the small town of Carolina, Puerto Rico. There were few Puerto Ricans playing baseball in the major leagues when Clemente was growing up. But Roberto recalls dreaming about it all the time.

"Baseball was my whole life," he says. "I would forget to eat because of baseball and one time my mother decided to punish me by burning my bat. But I got it out of the fire and saved it just in time."

While Clemente was still in high school, he signed a contract to play for Santurce, a team in the professional Puerto Rican League. He was 17 at the time and he received a bonus of $500 and one new baseball glove. His salary was $60 a month.

Soon, Clemente was the batting sensation of the Puerto Rican League and attracted the eye of several American teams. The Los Angeles Dodgers, then in Brooklyn, paid him a $10,000 bonus to sign with them. The rules for bonus players said that the Dodgers had to keep Roberto in the major leagues for two years. If he went to the minors any other team could buy him. But the Dodgers took a chance—they sent him to Montreal in the Triple A International League where they tried to hide his talents. They didn't want another major league team to see him and take him away. It was an experience Clemente never forgot.

"If I struck out I stayed in the lineup," he said. "If I played well, I was benched. One day I hit three triples and the next day I was benched. Another time they took me out for a pinch hitter with the bases loaded in the first inning."

But despite the Dodgers' attempts, Roberto didn't escape the notice of Pittsburgh Pirate scout Clyde Sukeforth. In November of 1954, the Pirates drafted Clemente, paying the ridiculous sum of $4,000 for him. The Dodgers were helpless—they had taken a chance and lost.

Clemente hit just .255 for the Pirates in his rookie season. Then came the first of a series of injuries and ailments which miraculously transformed Clemente into the superstar that he is. A back injury slowed down his swing and made him go with a pitch. His average jumped to .311 in 1956 but it was several years before he could perfect his style and consistently reach the .300 class.

Meanwhile, Clemente was developing a mutual love affair with Pittsburgh's win-starved fans. Often he would go to the ball park early and remain late, simply to chat with fans and sign autographs.

In 1960, Clemente hit .314 with 94 runs-batted-in and 16 home runs as the Pirates won the pennant and the World Series for the first time in 30 years. But Clemente did not attend the Pirates' World Series celebration. A friend found Roberto wandering in the Pittsburgh streets with the jubilant hometown fans.

"What are you doing here?" he asked. "Why aren't you back with the team?"

"I do not feel like a player now," Clemente replied. "See all these people? I feel like one of them. They are happy and I am happy and I want to be with them."

Roberto wasn't completely happy, however. He was disappointed that he did not get more credit for the team's victories. He was more determined than ever to prove himself in 1961. He did, winning his first batting title with a .351 average despite a painful elbow injury suffered when he was hit by a pitched ball at mid-season.

His back and arm continued to bother him in the early 1960s but his hitting remained unaffected. In 1964 he won his second batting crown with a .339 average. Then came one of his most serious illnesses. He caught malaria over the winter and was bedded down for weeks.

When spring training opened, Clemente was still weak and had lost 23 pounds. Yet, by the time the 1965 season was over, Clemente had claimed his second straight batting championship, this time with a .329 average.

Even though Clemente had established himself as one of the game's best hitters, he was criticized for failing to hit with power. Not once between 1955 and 1965 had Clemente driven in 100 runs a season. Only once during that time had he hit more than 17 home runs.

Clemente slides into second, trying to avoid being tagged by the Giants' Hal Lanier.

Before the 1966 season started, Pirate manager Harry Walker called Clemente aside.

"Bob," he said, "I know you could hit more homers if you tried. But you've always figured you're helping the club more by hitting for an average. This season, go for power and let's see what happens."

"Okay," Roberto said, "but I hope I don't hurt the team."

Clemente hurt nobody but opposing pitchers. When the season was over, his average had dipped to .317. But he had slammed 29 home runs, batted in 119 runs and led the Pirates in a pennant chase they lost the last weekend of the season. For his performance, he received the league's Most Valuable Player award.

The next year Walker told Clemente to shoot for a high average again. "Not too many men have ever won four batting titles," Walker told him, "but I think you can." Clemente's back bothered him again and so did a leg ailment. But he responded to Walker's urging by winning his fourth batting championship, hitting .357. He also

drove in 110 runs and blasted 23 homers.

Just before spring training opened in 1968, Roberto fell outside his home in Puerto Rico and injured his shoulder. Though he continued to play ball, his shoulder hurt so much he couldn't swing properly. He never fully recovered and finished the year with the lowest batting average in 10 years—.291.

In 1969, Clemente felt the need to prove himself again. He had to show everyone that the '68 season was a fluke. Even though the shoulder continued to bother him, Roberto played as if he were 10 years younger. He hit an amazing .345 and came within three points of winning his fifth batting title.

There is one word that best sums up Roberto Clemente's baseball life—pride. Pride made him continue to play even when his back or leg ached with pain. And pride made him always try to do better even after he had accomplished what few men had done. As a former teammate once said:

"Sure Robby is a proud man. But he's also one great baseball player."

A. J. FOYT

In 1935 auto mechanic Tony Foyt and his wife had a son. They named him Anthony Joseph Foyt, Jr., but always called him A. J. Tony was proud of the boy and he could hardly wait until A. J. was old enough to share Tony's one big passion—racing cars.

When A. J. was only three and a half, his father built him an electric-powered car. In the little car A. J. scooted all around the Foyts' neighborhood in Houston, Texas. When A. J. was six, his father built him his first gasoline-powered racer. It had four gears and could run up to 55 miles an hour. Tony took A. J. to a nearby stock-car track and let him run the car between races.

"I thought the car was the most beautiful thing there ever was," A. J. has recalled. "It was painted red and white. I wore a red silk racing outfit that my mother made for me. Boy, I thought I was something in those days."

Tony built the cars strictly for A. J.'s fun, never expecting that A. J. would want to make a career out of racing. Tony himself had driven stock cars and midgets around Houston and he knew first-hand that it was a dangerous business. But by the time A. J. was 18 he had made up his mind that racing was what he wanted.

For A. J., his choice of a career eventually paid off handsomely. He won the U. S. driving championship five times during the 1960s and won the Indianapolis 500 three times. By 1970 he had earned over a million dollars in prize money and millions more through endorsements of auto products.

During A. J.'s years of success, his wife Lucy and his father begged him to quit driving. They knew A. J. could make a fine living in racing without being a driver. They had seen too many drivers killed on the track, including some of A. J.'s friends. But A. J. refused to quit, and he refused to worry about the danger. "Put me in the middle of the pack at Indianapolis," A. J. said, "and I feel safer there than I do out driving on the highway."

The facts didn't quite bear A. J. out. In 1965 and '66 he was in three serious accidents. The first time, in a stock-car race at Riverside, California, his brakes failed. He plunged over a wall and a 35-foot embankment. He was pulled unconscious from the wreck with a broken back and right leg. His doctor said he would never race again.

But A. J. did come back, only to crash at the start of the 1966 Indy 500. Then, at Milwaukee, he smashed into a barrier and he was engulfed by a 20-foot-high wall of flames. By the time he had pried himself free of the car and the fire, 15 percent of his body had been burned. He had never known such agony. "Get me a hammer and hit me in the head with it!" he yelled to a member of his pit crew. "Put me out of my misery!"

Once the burns had healed, though, A. J. was back on the track as always. It didn't matter what kind of car he was driving— stock, midget, formula or Grand Prix— competition was what A. J. lived for.

A. J. seemed more concerned with winning than with the money he could earn. Shortly after he had won $117,000 at Indianapolis in 1961, A. J. put his life on the line to win a mere $600, and even paid $100 for the privilege. It happened at a rain-soaked, lumpy midget track in Terre Haute, Indiana. Only 24 cars were permitted to qualify, and A. J. had come in 25th in the qualifying heat.

A. J. Foyt zooms across the finish line to win the 1964 Indianapolis 500. He averaged over 147 miles per hour for the 500-mile race.

Foyt walked over to Dick Northam, the 24th qualifier, and said, "I'll give you $100 if you'll withdraw your car."

Northam looked at A. J., looked at the dangerous track and said, "Okay." A. J. entered the race, took the lead at the halfway point and never lost it.

This will to compete put A. J. in racing to start with. He began to race in 1953, after quitting Houston's Lamar High School in the 11th grade. When he was 20 he married blonde Lucy Zarr. He kept the marriage secret for three months before he got up the courage to tell his father.

After his son Anthony Joseph III was born, A. J. took his family on the racing circuit with him. Once A. J. and Lucy spent their last 50 cents on milk and toast for the baby and went hungry themselves.

Even in those early years, A. J. managed to save enough to get to Indianapolis on Memorial Day for the Indianapolis 500. At first he watched the race from the stands and dreamed of qualifying himself someday. "Those drivers made it look so easy I felt I could get out there and do as well," he said.

A. J. found out it was a little tougher than it looked. He qualified for the 500 for the first time in 1958. On the first lap of the race he was caught in the 12-car pileup that cost veteran Pat O'Connor his life. Foyt stayed in the race, but hit an oil slick on the 89th of the 200 laps. He slid 968 feet backwards before he got the car under control. He refused to quit, however, and finished 16th in the field of 33. In 1959 he finished tenth.

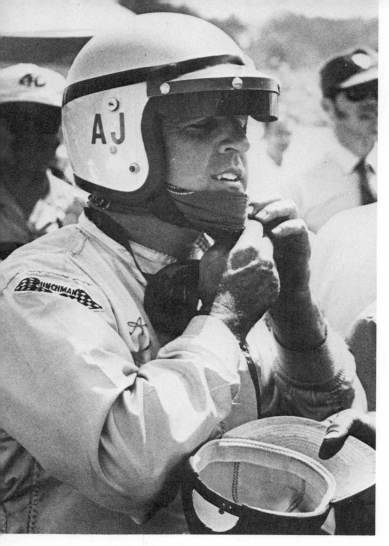

Foyt straps on his helmet, getting ready for a race.

A. J. seemed to have a good chance to win the 500 in 1960, but a bad clutch forced him out on lap 90. Although his loss seemed to put him hopelessly out of contention for the national big-car driving championship, he came on strong at the end of the season. He won four of the year's last six races and became, at age 25, the second youngest national champion ever.

In 1961, Foyt and favorite Eddie Sachs staged one of the most exciting duels in Indy 500 history. During the last 300 miles they battled back and forth for the lead. Afterward Sachs marveled at Foyt's competitiveness. "I would get four or five car-lengths ahead of him," said Eddie, "and suddenly

here he would go by me again—zoom—and I kept thinking, where in the devil is this guy coming from?"

With only six laps to go, Foyt had to make a fuel stop and it looked like Sachs would go on to win. But with three laps to go Sachs noticed his right-rear tire was worn dangerously thin and pulled into the pit. Foyt charged by just as Sachs was leaving the pit. He kept his lead and won by five seconds and became Indy's youngest winner. He also set a record for speed, averaging 139.130 miles per hour. A. J. had once said that if he won Indy he might quit driving. But his victory there only made him hunger for more.

The 1962 season was something of a disaster for the intense Foyt, even though he won over $100,000. He split up with his chief mechanic, George Bignoti, and was fined $1,000 for threatening a Milwaukee race promoter. He also lost his national title. But he won it back in '63 and '64, and won Indy again in '64, with a record speed of 147.350 mph.

Accidents slowed Foyt down the next two years, and in 1967 he wasn't expected to stand a chance at Indy against owner Andy Granatelli's controversial jet turbine car. Neither was anyone else. The car, driven by Parnelli Jones, had broken all the records in the qualifying heats.

True to form, Jones took a big lead through most of the race. Foyt was driving a rear-engine Ford Coyote which he himself had designed and named. He was in second place most of the day, but several laps behind Jones. Then, with Jones just three laps away from victory, a $6 ballbearing gave out in the turbine car. Parnelli was through for the day and A. J. was a winner again. He had gotten a lucky break, but his victory was well-deserved. His average speed of 151.207 mph was another record, and he joined the legendary Wilbur Shaw and Mauri Rose as the only three-time winners in Indy history.

Twelve days later A. J. continued to prove his driving mastery in a much different kind of race. Teaming with Dan Gurney, he entered the grueling Grand Prix at Le Mans, France. It is the world's most dangerous and difficult race, run over country roads for a full 24 hours. Entering the race for the first time, A. J. drove 14 of the 24 hours. Foyt and Gurney won the race, becoming the first American drivers to beat the Europeans on their home ground.

In the next two years A. J. became obsessed with the idea of being the first four-time winner at Indy. The 500 had always been his favorite race. "There's only one Indianapolis," he said. "It pays the biggest purse, it pulls the most drivers and it's the biggest challenge of them all. I don't care if you win it for the first time or the second or the third time. It's still the greatest feeling in the world."

In 1968 only five drivers finished the race. Foyt wasn't one of them, dropping out on the 86th lap. The next year, though, it looked like he might win again. He had the fastest qualifying time, at better than 169 mph. And for more than half of the race he was out in front. But then his manifold broke, requiring 22 minutes for repair. Mario Andretti breezed home, becoming an easy winner.

If A. J. had finally retired, no one could have blamed him. He was an extremely wealthy man, owning real estate and oil wells. "To be truthful," he said, "I don't have too much to drive for anymore except for the glory."

But for A. J. Foyt the glory was enough. He planned to keep right on racing, still hungry for the thrill of being the first man to pass the checkered flag of victory.

Foyt (lower left) crosses the finish to win his third Indianapolis in 1967. An accident has just occurred to the right of the pole.

BOB GIBSON

Bob Gibson was three years old, and he was very sick. The doctors said it was pneumonia. Bob's big brother Leroy wrapped him in a blanket and took him to the hospital. When they got there the sick little boy looked up at his brother and said, "Leroy, am I going to die?"

"Of course not," said Leroy, trying to hide his worry. "You're going to get well real quick, and just as soon as you do I'm going to get you a new baseball and a glove."

It took several months for Bob to recover fully. When he finally did, Leroy kept his promise. He got Bob the ball and glove, and they became Bob's favorite possessions. They were also among the few things that Bob could call his own.

The Gibsons were very poor. There were eight in the family and they lived in a four-room shack in a poor Negro neighborhood in Omaha, Nebraska. Once a rat bit Bob on the ear while he was sleeping. He owned one pair of shoes and used cardboard to keep water from seeping through the soles.

Bob's father had died of pneumonia a month before Bob was born on November 9, 1935. He was the seventh child in the family. Bob's mother worked in a laundry and as a cleaning woman, but her pay was low and every penny had to go far.

In the years after his bout with pneumonia, Bob had more than his share of other physical ailments. He developed rickets, a rheumatic heart, asthma and hay fever. But he refused to let these problems spoil his love for sports. At Omaha Technical High School he played basketball and baseball, and high-jumped on the track team. By graduation he was a healthy looking 6-foot-1, 180-pounder, and had attracted a major-league baseball scout.

He was offered $3,000 to sign a contract with the St. Louis Cardinals but Bob's brother Leroy convinced him he should go to college. Bob had already applied for a basketball scholarship to Indiana University, but had been turned down because the school said it had already filled its quota of Negroes.

Leroy helped Bob get a scholarship to Creighton University in Omaha. Bob lived at home and got a fine education as a philosophy major; and he was a standout athlete. He averaged over 20 points a game in basketball. In baseball he had a winning record as a pitcher, played centerfield and led his conference with a .340 batting average as a senior.

Bob left Creighton in 1957, six credits shy of his degree. He signed a $4,000 bonus with the Cardinals and played that year for minor league teams in Omaha and Columbus, Georgia. He had a blazing fastball, but he was wild and he didn't have a curve. His time with Columbus was the worst experience of his life. He learned for the first time what it could be like for a Negro in the South.

"I got a lot of static from the fans," he recalled, years later. "One fan called me 'Alligator Bait.' I laughed. I had no idea what he meant. Later, I found out. Negro kids used to be tied to the end of a rope and dragged through the swamps, to attract alligators. The Negro kid would be pulled out of the water and onto the shore, and the alligator would come out of the water after him. Then they'd catch the alligator. Alligator bait. That was what Negroes were good for, in Columbus."

Gibson was more effective the next year,

Bob Gibson shows his pitching form late in the 1968 season. The big Cardinal seems ready to fly as he falls toward first base.

pitching at Omaha and Rochester, New York. By the middle of 1959 he had earned a try-out with the Cardinals. He started his first major-league game on July 30, beating Cincinnati, 1–0. It was a great beginning, but Bob won only two more while losing five the rest of the season.

In 1960 and early in 1961 Gibson continued to have troubles. For one thing, he tended to put the ball over the middle of the plate instead of going for harder-to-hit strikes on the corner. Also, Bob's confidence was low because of the way Cardinal manager Solly Hemus was using him. "I'd start for a while, then I'd miss a turn," Bob said. "I never knew where I stood."

In July of 1961 Hemus was replaced by Johnny Keane, who was well aware of Gibson's problems. On the night Keane took over the team, he walked up to Bob in the clubhouse and handed him a ball. "Here," said the new manager, "you pitch."

Bob responded by beating the Dodgers, and even hit a home run. Johnny Keane kept Gibson in the rotation the rest of the season. Bob led the league in bases-on-balls that season but he also had a respectable 13–12 record. From then on Gibson was a Cardinal for good and he gave the biggest credit for his success to Keane.

"Johnny Keane believed in me," Gibson said. "When a man feels like that about you, you can do almost anything."

Gibson was also a vastly improved pitcher. He had refined his fastball and could hit the corners of the plate. He also had a strong curve, and a hard slider. His bases-on-balls total dropped while his strikeouts jumped to over 200 a season.

Late in the '62 season, a near-tragedy occurred. Bob was taking batting practice one day when his spikes caught in the dirt. Crack! The noise sounded like a twig snapping, and Bob felt a sharp pain. He had broken his left leg. His season was over, with a 15–13 record.

The leg healed over the winter, but Bob still worried about it early in the '63 season. He knew that the career of Dizzy Dean, the Cardinals' great pitcher of the 1930s, had been cut short because of a broken toe. But Gibson's worries were unfounded. He finished the season with an 18–9 record.

In 1964 Gibson was one of the key men for the Cardinals in one of the most exciting pennant races in baseball history. On August 15 the Cardinals trailed the Phillies by 9½ games. Up to that point Gibson had only a 10–10 record, largely because of a sore arm. But in the closing weeks of the season he showed the competitive spirit that he soon became famous for. He won nine of his last thirteen decisions. On the last day of the season he came out of the bullpen for the final four innings and helped the Cardinals clinch the pennant.

In the World Series against the Yankees Gibson pitched and lost the second game. In the fifth game, with the Series even at two games apiece, Gibson was a winner. The Cardinals took a 2–0 lead into the ninth inning. Mickey Mantle got on base on an error. The next batter, Joe Pepitone, smashed a line drive off Gibson's right buttock. Gibson, who falls toward first base after each pitch, took a few huge strides, scooped the ball and threw in the same motion. Pepitone was out.

The next Yankee batter, Tom Tresh, hit a home run. If Pepitone had been on base, the Yankees would have won, 3–2. Gibson's great fielding had saved the game. In the tenth inning catcher Tim McCarver won the game for St. Louis with a three-run homer.

The Cardinals lost the sixth game, so the Series would be decided by the seventh game. Even though Gibson had had only two days' rest, manager Johnny Keane wanted him to pitch it. Once again Keane's faith in Gibson was justified. Bob tired late in the game, giving up three home runs, but an early 6–0 lead had given him enough of a cushion. The Cardinals won, 7–5, taking their first World Series since 1946. The biggest hero was Gibson, who set a Series strikeout record of 31.

Gibson won 20 games in '65, and 21 the season after that. But in July of '67, Roberto Clemente drove a line drive off Bob's right leg, cracking the fibula. Amazingly, Gibson pitched to three more batters before coming out of the game. But after that he was lost to the Cardinals until September.

His chance of winning 20 games was ruined, but the Cardinals were very much in the thick of another pennant race. Once more Gibson proved almost unstoppable in the closing weeks. In September he won seven of his last nine games and the Cardinals were National League champions again.

In the World Series against the Boston Red Sox, Gibson was even stronger than he had been in '64, giving up only three runs in three games and limiting Boston to 14 hits. Gibson won the first, fourth and seventh games to make the Cardinals World Champs again. For the second time he was voted the Series' Most Valuable Player.

In 1968 Gibson had his finest season yet, and was voted the league's MVP. His record was 22–9 and his earned-run average was even more remarkable. He allowed just 1.12 runs a game, a record for baseball's modern era. The Cardinals won the pennant for the third time in five years, facing the Detroit Tigers in the World Series. Gibson was brilliant in the first game, too, but lost the seventh game when some of his teammates made fielding and baserunning mistakes. The Tigers won the game and the Series.

The following year the Cardinals fell from first place but Gibson won 20 or more games for the fourth time in five years. He

After beating the Red Sox in the seventh game of the 1967 World Series, Gibson is doused with champagne in the clubhouse.

finished at 20–13. New players for the Cardinals never failed to be impressed by Gibson's performance and by his spirit.

"I have never seen a pitcher more dedicated to baseball than Bob Gibson," said pitcher George Culver, when he joined the Cardinals for the 1970 spring training. "We stood in the outfield together the other day and he talked about his arm hurting him. He said it always hurt him but that he wasn't going to stop. He couldn't understand why so many pitchers refuse to pitch because their arms hurt. I learned something from him that day and a little bit each day after."

BOB HAYES

One day when Bob Hayes was a high school freshman, he was attending physical education class. The class was running races on a blacktop road. In a field next to the road the varsity track team was working out. One of Bob's friends pointed to a sprinter in the field and said he was the fastest man on the team.

"Is that right?" said Bob, not terribly impressed.

Later, the varsity sprinter came over to the road. Hayes went up to him and said, "You may be the fastest man on the team, but I can beat you."

The sprinter glared at Hayes, then looked him over. He couldn't believe it. Bob was only 5-foot-6 and weighed only 120 pounds. He looked as though a good breeze would blow him off the track. Of course the varsity man couldn't let the challenge pass unnoticed. An informal race was arranged right there, with everyone watching. When it was over, Bob Hayes had won, just as he said he would.

The varsity track coach was amazed, and excited at the prospect of working with Hayes in the years to come. "You've got 9.6 speed," he told Bob, referring to how fast he thought Bob could run the 100-yard dash. Bob didn't seem surprised. He had been confident about his speed since his grade school days, when he would race other kids in the street for a nickel a race. Bob never lost.

Bob began to grow when he was 16, and in a few years he reached 5-foot-11, and 185 pounds. His ankles and lower legs were strikingly thin, and his calves not very muscled. But his thighs bulged, and he had broad shoulders and a deep chest. He was not the lithe, classic sprinter. Pounding

Bob Hayes, a hero in two different sports, waits to get into the game for the Dallas Cowboys.

down the track, he looked more like a football player, which is why his fellow sprinters called him "the fullback." Yet with his unorthodox style he did far more than run the 9.6-second hundred as his coach had predicted. He set world records in three dash events and won a gold medal at the 1964 Tokyo Olympics.

As it turned out, Hayes *was* a football player too. He began playing at 16, and attended college on a football scholarship. After graduation he became a record-setting pass receiver with the Dallas Cowboys, and began making his mark in a second sport.

It takes a special kind of toughness to make it to the top in two different sports. Bob Hayes had that toughness. If he hadn't, he might not even have made it through life. He was born October 20, 1942, in a Jacksonville, Florida, black ghetto known as "Hell's Hole." Fighting was a way of life there. Bob didn't go looking for fights, but when he found himself faced with one, he usually relied on his fists, not his legs, to get him out of it. "A boy can't run from trouble," he has said.

Bob's parents separated when he was eight. He stayed with his mother, who supported him and his older brother Ernest by working as a domestic. Bob shined shoes for spending money. When he graduated from high school Bob accepted a football scholarship to Florida A & M, an all-black college famous for its football program directed by coach Jake Gaither.

In 1960, Bob's freshman year at Florida A & M, an incident came close to destroying his future. He went to a store one night with a friend. When a third student came along, Bob's friend pulled out a water gun, held it at the student's back and asked for his money. All the student had on him was six cents and a pack of gum. Bob thought the whole thing was a joke and just stood there watching. He didn't even know his friend had a gun. But when police came around the corner, Bob got scared and ran, forgetting his own advice about not running from trouble.

He escaped. But the next night the police came to his home. Bob was convicted of participating in the robbery, even though he had nothing to do with it except that he was present and then ran away. At first Bob was sentenced to ten years in jail but coach Gaither stepped in. "Give me this boy for four years," he told the court, "and you'll never have any trouble from him the rest of his life."

The sentence was suspended and Hayes was placed on ten years' probation. Then he moved in with coach Gaither and his wife. Gaither became like a father to Bob and Bob called Mrs. Gaither "Mama." Five years later Bob was granted a full pardon by Florida Governor Haydon Burns and Bob's "crime" was erased from the records.

Even though Bob loved football and was close to coach Gaither, it was track that brought him fame in college. The first time most people heard of him was in 1961, when he ran the 100-yard dash in 9.3 seconds, tying Jesse Owens' world record. One of the few races he lost in those four years came when he had 103 fever. Even then, he refused to use illness as an excuse and reacted strongly to losing. "I was humiliated," he has said. "It wasn't so much me, but the people who believed in me. I decided that day I never wanted to lose again."

Bob's determination from then on was fierce. When Frank Budd of Villanova lowered the record for the 100 to 9.2, Hayes came back to equal that mark and beat Budd face to face in some memorable races in 1962. The next year, running indoors for the first time in his life, Hayes set a world record of 6.9 seconds in the 70-yard dash, and 5.9 in the 60. Then, on June 21, in a semi-final heat in St. Louis, Hayes set a new 100-yard world record at 9.1 seconds. He clocked four more 9.1 dashes before he retired.

Bob put on his greatest show in the '64 Tokyo Olympics. He won a qualifying heat in the 100-meter dash in 9.9 seconds, faster

Hayes wins the 100-meter dash (above) during a meet between the U.S. and Germany. His huge thighs and barrel chest show why he was called "the fullback." During the 1964 Olympics (below), Hayes finishes first in a heat of the 400-meter relay. His great finishes helped the relay team win the gold medal.

than the world record. But the time was not officially recognized because of a slight tailwind. He won the finals in 10.0, tying the old world record. He placed the gold medal around the neck of his mother, who was in the stands.

Nine days later, Bob Hayes left the spectators speechless. He was running the anchor leg in the 400-meter relays. Bob's teammates ran and passed the baton poorly, and by the time Bob got the baton he was in sixth place, ten yards behind leader Jocelyn Delecour of France. But within 40 yards Hayes caught Delecour, and Bob went on to win by three yards.

"This is ridiculous," said assistant U. S. track coach Charlie Walter, looking at his stopwatch. "I got Hayes in 8.6."

"Yes, it's ridiculous," said head coach Bob Giegengack. "But it has to be true. Hayes had to do the impossible to win as big as he did from so far back."

Hayes, a world hero, returned to Florida A & M after the Olympics to play during the last half of the football season. He did so well that he was invited to a couple of allstar bowl games. He had been a running back under Jake Gaither, but in the North-South game he caught seven passes as a flanker, ran back punts and kickoffs and scored on a 39-yard run from scrimmage. Two weeks later, in the Senior Bowl, Hayes caught a 53-yard touchdown pass from Joe Namath to earn the South team a 7–7 tie.

Hayes went from his triumphs in post-season games to a spot with the Dallas Cowboys. Professional teams have often drafted sprinters on the chance that their speed would make up for other shortcomings. But many are too fragile for football and other cannot run in the broken field the way they ran on the straight track. Many spectators expected Bob to fail.

Bob found out he had plenty to learn in the pros. For one thing, he didn't really know how to catch the ball. He held his hands wrong and his thumbs got in the way. "He batted down the ball instead of catching it," said Dallas veteran receiver Buddy Dial. "He looked like he belonged on defense."

He also balked at the precision the pros demanded. One day in practice, assistant coach Red Hickey told Bob to run a pattern inside a linebacker. Bob could easily outrun the linebacker, but that wasn't what coach Hickey was asking. The pattern called for Bob to use moves and muscle, as well as speed, to outwit the linebacker.

Bob tried the maneuver several times, without success. "Coach," Bob finally said, "I can't get inside him."

"You have to," Hickey said.

"There's no way," Bob said.

"Find a way, or I'll send you home."

Bob was discouraged. He took his problem to Mama Gaither, but got no sympathy from her. "Coach Hickey is a good man," she said. "You're a professional now. You're not in college anymore."

Bob went back the next day and found that with hard work and concentration he *could* go inside the linebacker. And with more hard work in the weeks to follow, Hayes began adding other skills to his speed. By the beginning of the regular season, Bob was ready to take a place as one of the most exciting performers in pro football.

His first catch in the NFL came against the New York Giants. It went 37 yards, and would have gone for a touchdown if Hayes hadn't outrun his blockers. In his second game, against Washington, he got a touchdown when he fooled veteran cornerback Johnny Sample on a double sideline fake.

Hayes also impressed the pros with his willingness to block, and to make contact. On one play Bob crashed into Giant de-

fender Dick Lynch while Dallas receiver Frank Clarke was making the catch. "I didn't know you could hit like that," said Lynch, looking up at Hayes.

"You're on the ground, aren't you, baby?" said Hayes.

The Cowboys soon found that there was little Hayes couldn't do. "There's no doubt in my mind," said Red Hickey, "that if nothing physical happens to this boy, he will be one of the all-time greats. He has to be: he has the moves, he can catch in a crowd, he's durable, he's teachable, he's one of the most unaffected kids I've ever been around . . . and he runs the 100 in 9.1—or whatever he needs to."

The coach knew what he was talking about. By the end of the 1969 season Bob Hayes had completed five years in pro ball. In that time he had become the NFL's touchdown leader among active receivers, with 49. He also had the best average yardage per catch—19.4.

Bob's explosiveness on the field, and his easy-going nature off it, made him a favorite among the fans. They constantly wrote to him, and sought him out for autographs. One encounter with a couple of boys brought back special memories for Bob. After a game, a nine-year-old boy came up to him and said, "I'm running just like you, Bob. I think I can lick you." And another boy said, "Let's race, Bob."

Bob declined, but he couldn't help smiling. It brought back memories of another young boy who once thought he was pretty good and wasn't afraid to prove it. It had been a long time ago, but that young boy was still proving it, in every way.

Out ahead of the defense, Bob pulls down another pass for the Cowboys.

On the famous Green Bay Sweep, Paul Hornung follows his blocker Fuzzy Thurston, guiding Thurston by pulling on his shirt.

PAUL HORNUNG

The Green Bay Packers huddled under the goal posts, the ball on their 10-yard line. They led, 13–12, in this game against Cleveland for the 1965 championship of the National Football League. But the Browns, after a 28-yard field goal by Lou Groza, were rallying. The big Packer backs, trying to run on a mushy field, seemed glue-footed as they picked up small gains or no gains at all.

In the Packer huddle Paul Hornung looked around at his teammates, a grin flitting across his handsome face. "Hey, you guys," he said. "Hey, this is 1962 all over again."

The Packers had won their last championship in 1962. The Packer veterans grinned, remembering that past glory. "All at once," guard Fuzzy Thurston said later, "you could feel everybody in the huddle come up. All at once we didn't just think we could win. We *knew* we could win."

Green Bay pushed to midfield. On a third-down play, quarterback Bart Starr faked a hand-off to fullback Jim Taylor and gave the ball to halfback Paul Hornung.

The slim-hipped Hornung wiggled through a hole in the line, artfully following the big Packer blockers. Hornung seemed to skim above the muddy field, running under control to keep behind his wedge of blockers. He picked his way 20 yards before a Brown tackler bowled him over. A little later, with the ball on the Cleveland 13, Starr called for the famous Green Bay power sweep. Hornung took the ball, turned the right corner, and dashed down the sideline into the end zone for the winning touchdown. The Packers had won the 1965 championship.

No pro football team won more big games and more championship games during the 1960s than the Packers. From 1960 through 1967 they won the NFL's Western Conference title six times, and in five of those years they were NFL champions. No Packer player won more big games than Hornung. He was great in regular-season games, but was devastating whenever the Packers had to win a crucial game. And in championship games, time after time, he was the game's Most Valuable Player or leading ground gainer.

He gave the Packers more than yardage: he gave them leadership and poise. In 1963 Paul did not play, suspended because he had bet on football games. The Packers finished second in their division. "There was a little leadership lacking last season," Packer coach Vince Lombardi said when Hornung returned to the team for the 1964 season. "Maybe I shouldn't say that, but I think there was."

"Paul's a leader," linebacker Dan Currie said at the time. "He's not the kind of guy who would be a captain. He's not serious enough, he's always kidding around. What he has is a different kind of leadership. He never panics. He never loses his poise. No matter what the situation he's got that great confidence in himself. And he transmits that confidence to the other players."

During his peak years as a runner and a field-goal kicker, Paul often led the NFL in scoring. In 1960 he set an NFL record for

Although most famous as a runner, Hornung was also a kicker. Here he scores a field goal against the Detroit Lions in 1961.

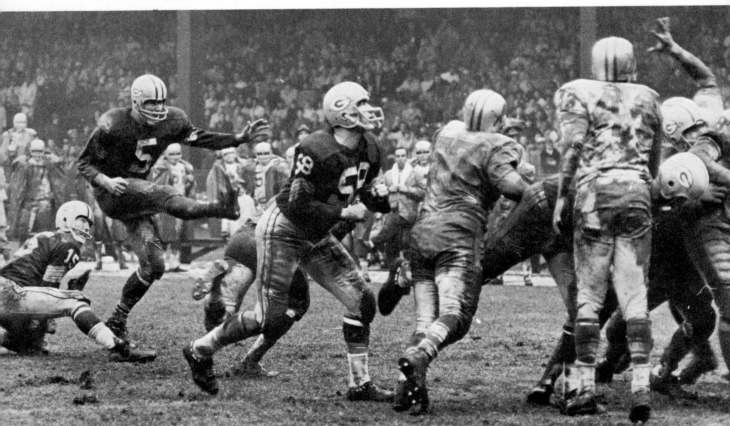

scoring in one season with 176 points—15 touchdowns, 15 field goals, and 41 conversions. He led the league again in scoring in 1961 and was leading in 1962 when a knee injury hobbled him. In 1960 and 1961 he was the league's Most Valuable Player.

But what Paul did best was scoring for the Packers when they needed most to score. He was the hero of the Packers' 1961 championship victory over the Giants, gaining 136 yards; in that game he set a playoff game record by scoring 19 points as the Packers won, 37–0. In a game against the Colts in 1965 that the Packers had to win, he scored five of the team's six touchdowns in a 42–27 victory. In a playoff against the Colts for the 1965 Western Conference title, he scored the Packers' only touchdown in a 13–10 victory. And in the 1965 championship game against Cleveland, he gained 105 yards in 18 carries, and was the game's leading rusher in the Packers' 23–12 victory.

"In that kind of game you just throw caution to the wind," Paul said later. "You've got to go into a game like that and forget about the little hurts because you'll have a chance to rest anyway. In the championship game you play more recklessly."

He paused, running a hand through his wavy blond hair. "This game is more mental than physical," he said. "Every club is loaded with guys who have something physically or they wouldn't be here. It's the guys who are right mentally who come out on top. It's the guys who don't make the big mistakes who win.

"Maybe that's why I do well in big games. When the pressure's on, guys get tight. By my very nature I'm a loose character. I'm not great physically, so I've had to learn to use what I have intelligently, to avoid mistakes.

"In the big game I make less mistakes than some other guy. Lombardi has won

with us because he's trained us to avoid big mistakes. We may fumble at midfield, but we don't fumble on the one.

"I try just as hard in every game . . . but I guess I just can't get up as high when the stakes aren't high."

When the stakes aren't high—a betting term. Paul was a bachelor for a long time and had a playboy's reputation for enjoying a glamorous life off the field. His life included parties, beautiful girls—and gambling. But the gambling caught up with him in 1963.

Hornung had been found guilty by NFL commissioner Pete Rozelle of betting on football games. Rozelle said, "There was no evidence that Hornung ever bet against his team, sold information for betting purposes, or performed less than his best in any game." But pro football players are forbidden to bet on games. "I did wrong," Hornung said. "And I deserve to be punished."

In March of 1964 his year-long suspension was lifted. Lombardi told Paul to come to Green Bay early to get in shape. "The Old Man wanted me to start in mid-April," Hornung told friends, "and I wanted to start the first of May. So we compromised. I started in mid-April."

It was Lombardi who had turned Hornung, a seeming flop, into a pro star. Paul had been a star in college and in high school, one of those people who turns everything he touches into gold. In fact, a Kentucky sportswriter nicknamed him The Golden Boy when the blond 17-year-old Paul led Louisville's Flaget High School to the 1952 state championship.

The Golden Boy went to college in South Bend, Indiana, to play for legendary Notre Dame. In his sophomore year, grown to 6-foot-2 and 215 pounds, he played fullback and numbed linemen with his plunges into the line. As a junior, he played quarterback

Hornung rests on the sidelines during the 1965 Championship game against Cleveland.

and led Notre Dame to an 8–2 record, confounding opponents who could never tell if he was going to run or pass. In his senior year as quarterback of a poor team that won only two games, Paul nevertheless won the 1956 Heisman Trophy as college football's player of the year.

Paul was the Packers' first draft choice. They tried him at quarterback but he wasn't accurate enough as a passer for pro football. And he wasn't fast enough as a fullback to get through a hole before it was plugged shut by a linebacker. The Golden Boy seemed to be one of those in-between players—great in college, not great enough for the pros.

Then along came Vince Lombardi in 1959, taking over a Packer team that had won only one game in 1958. "This year you are going to sink or swim at left halfback," Lombardi told Paul.

Paul soon mastered the left halfback job. He was especially effective on the pass-run option, rolling out on what looked like an end run, drawing in the defense, then lobbing a pass to an open receiver. He played brilliantly in 1959, the Packers winning seven of 12 games. In 1960 he led the league in rushing and the Packers won their first Western Conference title.

For the next six years the Packers were either first or second in the NFL West. In 1966, bothered by a pinched nerve in his shoulder, Hornung played only sporadically as the Packers won another NFL title and beat the Kansas City Chiefs in the first Super Bowl. Paul was traded to the New Orleans Saints in the expansion draft and retired in 1967 rather than begin again with a new team.

He served for a time as an assistant coach for the Saints, then became a broadcaster of pro football games in Chicago. But his exploits on the field will not be forgotten in Green Bay. "There may be better football players," Lombardi once said of Paul. "There may be fellows who run or pass better. But there are not many who do as many things as well as he does. And there is no one any better when the goal-line is at hand."

BOBBY HULL

In the spring of 1959, a team composed of mostly New York Rangers and a few Chicago Black Hawks made a tour of Europe. They played exhibition hockey games wherever they went. It was a pleasant trip, but New York's general manager Muzz Patrick couldn't wait for it to end. There was one young Black Hawk player on the tour that he wanted for the Rangers—at almost any price.

As soon as the plane landed in New York, Patrick rushed to a phone to call general manager Tommy Ivan of the Black Hawks. "Your players fit in real well with us in Europe," Patrick said. "I've got a proposition for you. Bathgate and Gadsby for Litz and Hull."

On the surface it sounded like a great trade for the Black Hawks. The Hawks would get Andy Bathgate, who had just been selected the National Hockey League's Most Valuable Player, and Bill Gadsby, who was a perennial All-Star. The Hawks would give up Ed Litzenberger, who had been the NHL's fifth leading scorer that season but was getting old. The fourth player was 20-year-old Bobby Hull, who had scored 31 goals in his first two years in the league.

The Chicago general manager wasn't fooled. "Nice try, Muzz," Tommy Ivan said, "but you know better than to ask for Hull. I wouldn't give you Hull for your whole team."

Within a few months Bobby Hull showed

Bobby Hull, the Golden Jet, clears the puck off the boards for the Black Hawks.

Hull (on right) moves toward the net from the corner against the New York Rangers.

exactly why everyone wanted him. During the 1959–60 season he scored 39 goals, led the league in total scoring and was second only to Gordie Howe in the voting for the Most Valuable Player. Since Hull was only 21, such accomplishments promised even more for the future. And in the years that followed, Bobby more than fulfilled his promise.

Hull, who became known as the "Golden Jet," brought a new kind of excitement to hockey. The mere presence of this blond-haired, powerfully muscled figure on the ice seemed to send currents of electricity through the crowds. When he began his charge with the puck, the crowd would roar in anticipation. They knew that no man

traveled with a puck as fast as Bobby Hull, and they knew when he began to wind up for his famed slapshot that the puck would soon be speeding toward the goal at up to 120 miles an hour.

If Hull excited the fans, he terrified NHL goalies. "I have to say I'm frightened by him," Los Angeles goalie Gerry Desjardins once said. "Of course there isn't one goaltender around who isn't scared. He shoots the puck anywhere—low, high. He admits himself he's terrified of his own shot. Even if you do stop the shot you're apt to get a bruise. Usually when a guy gets a breakaway on me I don't know who it is; I just don't pay attention to the guy. But when it's Bobby Hull, I know."

What scared the goalies most was that Hull's shots were often impossible to follow. The first time Oakland goalie Gary Smith faced Hull, Bobby got off a slapshot from center ice. Smith started to stick up his hand to stop the shot and was amazed when the puck hit the back of his glove. "The puck was already on its way *out* of the net," said Smith. "I felt like picking up the puck and saying, 'That's it for me.'"

Hull's power came from his boxer-like physique. He stood 5-foot-10, and weighed 191 pounds. His waist was 32 inches, but he needed custom-made sport jackets because his chest was 44 inches. His huge thighs were the pistons that enabled him to travel with the puck at such speed—he was once timed at nearly 30 miles an hour.

Bobby inherited some of his basic strength, and further developed it through hard work. He was born on January 3, 1939, in Point Anne, Ontario, and was one of 11 children. When he was seven years old, he could lift his father, who weighed 210 pounds, off the floor on his back. When he was eight, he started developing his arm and back muscles by chopping trees in the nearby woods. "I also walked to and from school four miles a day," he has said, "and during the winter I shoveled snow from morning till night."

Bobby was taught to skate by his sisters before he was three. When he got older he would get up at five in the morning and practice his skating before school. He began playing organized hockey at the age of ten, and was signed by the Black Hawks when he was 13 to play junior hockey. He played for several Chicago farm teams, finally ending with St. Catharines, which was about 200 miles from his home. His parents would often drive in to watch him play.

Bobby also played football with the high school team. One afternoon he scored two touchdowns in a scrimmage. When he got home for dinner, he found out that the Black Hawks, who trained in St. Catharines, wanted him to play that night in an exhibition game against the Rangers. Bobby bolted down his food, rushed over to the rink, and scored two goals against the Rangers. That night he was signed to a major-league contract, at the age of 18.

Bobby still had two years of eligibility left in junior hockey, and the people in St. Catharines were upset that the Hawks were "stealing" him away. But their anger soon turned to pride when Bobby proved himself so quickly in the NHL.

"The thing that amazes me," said Ranger coach Alf Pike, "is Hull's all-around ability. He can shoot the puck, he can slap it, he can draw the goaltender, he can shift, he can stickhandle. And he can hit. When he barrels into those corners, he usually gets the puck."

One of the few lessons Bobby had to be taught was that a fight doesn't do him or his team much good. He got into a stick-swinging battle with Lou Fontinato of the Rangers and drew an automatic $100 fine. "It was really foolish," Bobby said, "but I learned. I'm not getting paid to get thrown out of games."

Bobby made his first big headlines in the 1959–60 season, when he pulled off the hat trick (scoring three goals in one game) three times in three weeks. Two months later he scored four goals in a game. In the last game of the season he scored a goal and made an assist to bring his scoring total to 81 points, winning the league title.

Two seasons later Bobby tied the record of 50 goals set by Maurice Richard. In hockey that record was equivalent to baseball's 60 home runs. As it turned out, Bobby should have been credited with 51 goals. In one game against Detroit, Bobby shot the puck, but the official scorer also saw Bobby's teammate, Ab McDonald, swing his stick, and he credited McDonald with the goal. Later, after talking to other players, the official scorer admitted he had made a mistake. But league president Clarence Campbell wouldn't give Bobby the extra goal.

It seemed only a matter of time before Bobby would break the old record. But the next season wasn't it. Bobby scored only 31 goals and Bobby and the other Black Hawks were handicapped by disagreements with coach Rudy Pilous. "They worked us to death in training camps," said Bobby. "We played 17 exhibitions and had two tough practices a day. I was sick of hockey when the season started."

The next year Pilous was replaced by Billy Reay. And the year after that—1964–65—it looked as if Bobby would break the record with plenty to spare. In one stretch he had 35 goals in 37 games. But later in the season other teams began using effective tactics to stop him. "It's not that Bobby isn't playing well enough to score 51 or 61 goals," said general manager Tommy Ivan. "He's just not being allowed to play his game. He's hooked and held and tripped more than any man in the league."

Bobby was such a gentleman about the rough treatment he received that he was awarded the Lady Byng trophy for sportsmanship. But the next season he got a little tired of the way opposing teams assigned a special player to stick to him. So he began retaliating. He started racking up penalties, but he also was breaking loose for the goals.

Hull moves down the ice with the puck. When he gets within range he may send the puck toward the goal at speeds of 100 miles per hour or more.

He got 39 goals in his first 41 games. All he needed was 12 goals in the last 29 games to break the record.

It still wasn't as easy as it sounded. Bobby was sidelined for a time with a knee injury, and then he hurt his right hand in a fight against Detroit. Still, on March 2, he got goal No. 50. Now the pressure was on, and the Black Hawks seemed to feel it. Nobody on the team, including Bobby, scored a single goal in the next three games.

On March 12, Chicago played New York, and through the first two periods the Black Hawks were still scoreless. But at 2:57 of the third period, Chico Maki took a pass from Hull and scored. The entire Chicago team seemed relieved of the pressure.

Two minutes and 37 seconds later, Bobby picked up the puck about halfway down the ice. He cut toward center ice, and as defenseman Jim Neilson started to move toward Bobby, Hull slapped his shot from about 50 feet out. It was low and to the right side of the net. Black Hawk Eric Nesterenko cut across the goal, and as Ranger goalie Cesare Maniago reached out with his stick, the puck slid under Maniago's left glove and into the net.

The red light went on in the goal, and the Chicago fans went wild. They covered the ice with hats and cups and paper plates labeled "51." The ovation lasted seven and a half minutes; meanwhile, Bobby shook hands with his teammates and went over to the side of the rink to kiss his wife.

Bobby scored three more goals during the season and wound up with 54 goals and 97 total points. Three years later, in 1968–69, Bobby broke his own record by scoring 58 goals, but the new record didn't seem to mean as much. The schedule had been increased from 70 games to 74 games and the league had been expanded from six teams to 12. Scoring came easier against the

Hull sits on the sidelines.

weak expansion teams, and a new era of higher scoring was beginning.

During the last seasons of the 1960s, Bobby threatened to retire. He would stay away from training camp for several weeks, insisting on a larger salary. The Black Hawks knew Bobby could make good his threat, because he owned a large cattle ranch and could become a full-time rancher if he had to. But eventually they would reach an agreement and Bobby would continue to thrill fans wherever he played. Both on and off the ice he was an important public relations man for the sport, attracting new fans to the game and extending its popularity to new parts of the continent.

Everyone hoped he would play for a long, long time—everyone except opposing goalies. "When Bobby announced he was retiring at the start of the season," said Cesare Maniago in late 1968, "I told my wife I was sorry to see him go, because he was good for the game in general. But as far as goaltenders are concerned, it would have been a big relief for us."

DAVID "DEACON" JONES

In September 1969 the Los Angeles Rams of the NFL were getting ready for an exhibition game with the San Diego Chargers of the AFL. The Rams had lost to the Chargers the year before, 35–13, and they wanted revenge. "Don't worry," David "Deacon" Jones told his Rams teammates. "We'll pay them back."

"I hope so," someone said.

"What do you mean you *hope* so?" Jones said. "When the Deacon says something, bank on it. If the Deacon says an elephant is going to lay an egg, don't sit around wondering about it. Get out the skillet."

The Rams won, proving once again that it was unwise to doubt Deacon Jones's word, especially when he was on the defense, making his predictions come true. In the middle and late 1960s, the Rams' defensive left end was nearly unstoppable. And he was usually heading for the man with the ball. In one game against the Green Bay Packers he dropped quarterback Bart Starr four times for losses. "He was in on me so quickly," Starr said later, "that I thought he was one of my own backs."

Jones had tremendous speed for a man standing 6-foot-5 and weighing 250 pounds. He also had strength, intelligence, pride and the desire to hit his opponents on the football field. The combination brought him All-Pro honors five straight years, beginning in 1965. Teammate Merlin Olsen, an All-Pro tackle himself, was so awed by Jones that he once said, "I suspect that there has never been a better football player than Deacon Jones."

Jones got the nickname "Deacon" in college, where he would lead prayers before a game. Once, when some opposing players noticed Jones kneeling, one of them asked, "What's *he* praying for?"

"That he doesn't kill anybody," another player answered.

The Deacon's fame reached its peak when he became a part of the Rams' Fearsome Foursome. That was the name given to the defensive line composed of Jones at left end, Olsen at left tackle, Rosey Grier at right tackle, and Lamar Lundy at right end. Many experts considered the Fearsome Foursome the finest front four in history. The four helped make the Rams a top contender during the late 1960s.

By 1969, Jones was 31 and just approaching the top of his form. "Maturity in pro football often comes late," he said. "It takes a long time to learn the game."

No one knows better than Deacon Jones how long and hard the road is to pro football success. He was born on December 8, 1938, in Eatonville, Florida, a tiny black ghetto outside Orlando. He had two brothers and five sisters. The large family was a big financial burden on their father, Ishmael, who was a carpenter and handyman. To help out, young David took all the odd jobs he could find. In between jobs he played baseball, basketball, football and ran in track at Hungerwood High School in Orlando.

After graduating from high school, Deacon accepted a scholarship to tiny Mississippi Vocational College because freshmen there were permitted to play varsity sports. After one year he transferred to South Carolina State College, where he played defensive tackle and offensive end. He could run the 100-yard dash in 9.7 and once took a pass 75 yards for a touchdown. Another time he kicked a 48-yard field goal.

Despite his college accomplishments, the pros discovered him by accident. During his senior season, 1960, Rams scouts were run-

Deacon Jones leaps to knock down the pass as his teammates swarm around Detroit quarterback Milt Plum during a 1966 game.

ning through some college films to check the performance of a running back in a game against South Carolina State. In one sequence the running back was flat on his back and a South Carolina State tackle was sitting on his chest. "Who's the big kid?" said one of the scouts. They soon found out: Deacon Jones. A few weeks later the Rams drafted Jones in the 14th round.

When he reported to camp he wanted to play defensive end but quickly saw that the Rams had strong starters at that position. When the Rams asked what he played, he lied and said, "offensive tackle," because he knew they didn't have many of those. But before the season began, a regular defensive end, Gene Brito, got seriously ill. Jones started the 1961 season at Brito's position and became a regular from then on, playing in every game through the rest of the 1960s.

The early games weren't easy for Jones. He didn't know much more than the basics of the game. Sometimes he found himself running into his own linemen. And the Rams were a poor team in the early '60s,

Jones rests on the bench (left) while the offensive unit is on the field. Back in the game (right), he collars Green Bay quarterback Zeke Bratkowski.

finishing last in their division a couple of times. "You have to have a lot of pride just to show up," Jones said.

In 1963 Deacon made it even harder on himself by showing up at training camp at 290 pounds, forty pounds over his playing weight. But Jones eventually took off the weight and regained his speed and stamina. In 1964 he made 79 unassisted tackles, nearly a record.

The Deacon's quickness became legendary. In one game he chased after Pittsburgh ballcarrier Marv Woodson, who had a 20-yard lead, and brought him down from behind. "Oh, no, baby," said Marv to the 250-pound lineman. "Say it's not you."

"It's me, baby, it's me," said the Deacon.

Jones could be slowed down, but never for very long. Not even by injury. At various times he played with an ulcerous eyeball, a broken nose and a cracked spine. Against the Packers in 1968 he dislocated and split open his thumb when he got it caught on a Packer helmet. "It was agony," he said later. "I never felt such pain." Yet

he kept playing that day and twice he crashed into Packer ballcarriers to cause fumbles and help the Rams win the game.

In 1967, '68 and '69 the Rams came close to winning Western championships in the NFL, but they always seemed to fail in the big game. The loss of the title in 1969 was particularly bitter for Jones. The Rams had an outstanding season, winning all but two of their games. In the play-off for the Western Conference championship, the Rams were slight favorites but lost to the Minnesota Vikings, 23–20. In disappointment, Jones considered retiring but soon changed his mind. "I'll play till I'm 90—until we get the championship," he said.

He showed his determination in a spectacular game against Dallas the following week in the Playoff Bowl, a consolation game between the losers of the conference playoffs. Although the game had little significance, Jones went all-out as usual and was named the game's Most Valuable Defensive Player, a fitting tribute to a man who doesn't know how to give up.

HARMON KILLEBREW

Harmon Killebrew walked up to the plate in a game early in 1959. Killebrew was not quite 23 years old, but already he was a fearsome sight to a pitcher. Although he was only 5-foot-11, he weighed over 200 pounds. His huge shoulders, chest and thighs bulged through the flannel of his Washington Senators uniform. When he swung the bat, the veins and muscles in his arms seemed ready to burst through his skin.

Killebrew had started his major league career with a home run on opening day of 1959. Many more were to follow in the next month and a half, some of them so long they were nearly out of sight. One shot, in Washington, had come within two rows of clearing the entire ballpark.

Opposing pitchers knew they had a dangerous new man to worry about. They were determined to test him and see just how tough he was. Now Harmon was facing one of baseball's toughest competitors, veteran Frank Lary of the Detroit Tigers. Harmon, a righthanded hitter, swung a couple of times across the plate as Lary went into his windup. Lary threw and the ball headed straight for Killebrew's head. Harmon spun out of the way of the pitch and sprawled into the dirt.

Killebrew was shaken, but he knew that if he was to stay in the major leagues he must not be intimidated. He would have to get back in the batter's box and swing for all he was worth. Lary's next pitch came in for a strike, but Harmon never let it settle into the catcher's glove. He socked it far into Detroit's leftfield bleachers. The next time up he hit another home run that went just as far. Harmon Killebrew had given notice that no one was going to frighten him away.

By the end of May, Killebrew had 15 home runs. Washington hadn't had a baseball hero like this in many years. The excitement even spilled over into the White House. President Dwight D. Eisenhower made a rare trip to the ballpark. The President asked the young slugger to autograph a baseball for his grandson, David.

Killebrew kept up his home-run hitting the rest of the year, leading the American League with 42 for the season. It was a preview of the slugging he was to do all during the '60s. By 1969 he had won five more

Harmon Killebrew puts all his weight behind a mighty swing at the ball.

Although nicknamed "Killer," Killebrew is a mild man both on and off the field.

league home-run titles. He had also hit 40 or more home runs in seven different years, something only Babe Ruth had done before. Even more amazing was Killebrew's home-run frequency. Through the 1960s, Killebrew averaged one home run for each 12.7 times at bat. Only Ruth had done better with an average of 11.8.

Because of Harmon's ability to murder a baseball he became known early in his career as "Killer" Killebrew. But no ballplayer ever had a nickname that was less suited to his personality. Harmon was mild and soft-spoken, and as unassuming as the small town he grew up in.

He was born on June 20, 1936, in Payette, Idaho, a town of 4,500. Some of Harmon's strength traced back to his grandfather, who was supposedly the heavyweight wrestling champion of the Union Army dur-

ing the Civil War. Harmon's father also was an athlete, and was selected to a college All-America football team as a fullback.

Harmon was a T-formation quarterback at Payette High School, and graduated in 1954 with a B-plus average. He seemed headed for Oregon University on a football scholarship, but fate intervened. U. S. Senator Herman Welker had his law office in Payette and was a friend both of the Killebrews and of Washington Senators' owner Cal Griffith. Senator Welker suggested that Griffith send a scout to Payette to take a look at young Killebrew's powerful hitting.

Washington farm director Ossie Bluege came out to Idaho and saw Killebrew play three games. Harmon came to bat 12 times and hit five home runs, three triples, two doubles and two singles. One of the homers was so long that Bluege paced it off himself. It measured 450 feet.

A short time later Bluege went to Harmon's mother and asked permission to talk to her son. She agreed and sent Bluege to the schoolhouse which Harmon was painting to earn extra money.

Bluege found Harmon up on a scaffolding. When Harmon began climbing down to talk to him, Bluege was amazed by the size of Harmon's shoulders. "Here comes another Jimmy Foxx," Bluege thought, remembering the great Red Sox slugger of the '30s.

Bluege offered Killebrew a bonus contract for $30,000, which Harmon signed 11 days before his 18th birthday. By the middle of that summer Harmon was in Washington, sitting on the Senators' bench. Baseball rules at the time required that anyone receiving a bonus of over $6,000 had to spend two years in the majors before he could be sent down to the minors.

It was painfully obvious that Harmon needed some minor-league seasoning. He was too young, too inexperienced. Manager Bucky Harris watched Harmon work out in the infield and moaned, "My God, he throws like a girl!"

Harmon hit nine home runs during his two-year "sentence," before being sent down to Charlotte in mid-1956. Between '56 and '58 Harmon shuttled back and forth from the minors to the Senators. Once, in 1957, he thought he had made the Senators for good. But as the team boarded an airport bus in Cleveland during a rainstorm, a team official gave him the bad news. "You'll have to get your bag off this bus, Harmon," he said. "They're sending you to Chattanooga."

Harmon got off and began looking for his bag. "Look," said third-baseman Eddie Yost, "you'll get soaked. We'll get you a cab."

"No thanks," said Killebrew. "I guess I'd just as soon walk." And he trudged away through the rain, deeply disappointed.

But Killebrew refused to remain disappointed for long. He worked long hours trying to improve, and he was smart enough to follow and remember advice. Finally, in 1959, the Senators traded Eddie Yost to Detroit and Harmon came up to Washington to play third base.

Once Harmon began slugging his home runs, everyone knew he belonged in the majors. Harmon hit 28 homers by early July. During the second half of the season he hit only 14. Cal Griffith knew the problem was a natural one. Harmon had become a celebrity overnight and had to adjust to the attention he received.

In 1960 Killebrew suffered the first of a series of nagging injuries that would plague him from time to time during his career. He hit only 31 homers but his average picked up from .242 to .276.

The next year the original Senators moved west and became the Minnesota Twins. It was a change that seemed to bring out the best in Killebrew. He hit 46 home runs in 1961. In 1962 he led the league with 48 homers and 126 runs batted in.

The home runs continued to come—45 in 1963, 49 in 1964. But now Harmon began to get abuse as well as cheers from the fans. They hooted at his slowness afoot, booed him when he struck out and started calling him "Harmless Harmon." They also criticized him in '64 for his weak throws, not realizing he was playing with an injured arm that he didn't want other teams to know about.

In 1965 Killebrew showed the kind of unselfishness that had marked his entire career. Manager Sam Mele asked him to cut down on his swing to reduce his strikeouts. Harmon agreed. Killebrew knew the change would mean fewer home runs, but it might also mean more game-winning hits.

Mele also agreed that Harmon would play first base all season. In the past he had moved around, playing third and first, and the outfield. The Twins got off to a fast start and were in first place through the first months of the season. The pressure began to mount as teams started taking the Twins seriously. Harmon was keeping his end of the bargain by cutting down on his swing, and Mele was sticking to his promise of leaving Harmon at first base.

Harmon soon realized that Mele's promise was forcing him to leave first-baseman Don Mincher on the bench. Mincher was weak against lefthanded pitching but tough against righthanders. One night, with the Twins scheduled to face a righthander, Harmon approached Mele. "I know you would like to get Mincher's bat into the game," Killebrew said. "I'll play another position so Don can play first base, if it will help."

"What about my promise?" asked Mele.

"Forget it," said Harmon.

Killebrew is congratulated by a teammate after hitting a home run against the Yankees.

Killebrew went to left field that night. Later in the season he played third when the Twins faced righthanders and first when the pitching was lefty. "Harmon's volunteering to move from first base was an inspiration to every player," Mele said later.

Harmon was also inspiring at the plate. By the end of July he had driven home the winning run in the last inning five different times. Five other times he had tied games in the late innings and the Twins had finally won. His batting average with runners on second or third was .373.

On August 2 Harmon dislocated his left elbow in a collision at first base. He was out for a month. When he returned in September the Twins were still leading the league. He helped inspire them with his presence down the stretch to the pennant. Killebrew finished the season with just 25 home runs and a .269 batting average, but

manager Mele knew this was one case where statistics told little.

"Harmon, you're still the best home run hitter in the game," Mele said to him, "but you're also a team ballplayer, and in my book that's the biggest title there is."

The Twins met the Los Angeles Dodgers in the World Series. In the deciding seventh game Harmon almost helped pull it out for the Twins. Sandy Koufax held a 2–0 lead over the Twins with one out in the ninth inning. Harmon hit a line-drive single, which brought the tying run to the plate. But Koufax struck out the next two batters and the Dodgers had won the Series.

After that season Harmon was told to go for home runs again, and he obliged by hitting 39 and 44 the next two years. He hit only 17 homers in 1968 because he was out much of the season. During the All-Star game, he had stretched for a low throw at first base and ruptured the hamstring muscle in his left leg.

Harmon came back strong for the 1969 season, playing in all 162 games. He also had his finest and most satisfying season ever. He tied his personal high with 49 home runs and batted in 140 runs, more than ever before. And most amazing of all, he stole eight bases—one more than he had stolen previously in his entire career.

Opponents showed their respect for Killebrew by walking him 145 times. And the baseball writers showed their regard by voting him the American League's Most Valuable Player. He was the biggest reason the Twins won the league's Western Division.

A few years before, catcher Earl Battey summed up very well Killebrew's value to Minnesota. "This team without Killebrew," said Battey, "is like a man dressed up for a formal affair with white tie and tails and wearing muddy shoes. Harmon puts us all in bigger shoes and adds the sparkle."

SANDY KOUFAX

It was October, 1963, a sunny early-October afternoon in Yankee Stadium, which was decked out in bunting. More than 69,000 fans had come to see the opening game of the World Series between the New York Yankees and the visiting Los Angeles Dodgers. Two of the greatest lefthanded pitchers of all time, Whitey Ford of the Yankees and Sandy Koufax of the Dodgers, would be facing each other.

In the first inning, Koufax struck out Tony Kubek on a curve ball and Bobby Richardson on a fast ball and caught Tom Tresh watching on a curved third strike. In the second inning, after John Roseboro's home run had helped the Dodgers to a 4–0 lead, Koufax faced Mickey Mantle. He threw two curve strikes, then drilled a fast ball past him. Then he got Roger Maris swinging on another fast ball for his fifth straight strikeout, tying a World Series record.

The fans in Yankee Stadium cheered the slender Dodger pitcher as though he were one of their own. To some extent he was, having grown up in Brooklyn and having begun his baseball career with the old Brooklyn Dodgers before they moved to Los Angeles.

Elston Howard ended Sandy's strikeout streak by fouling out, but Sandy added another strikeout in the third inning and three more as he struck out the side in the fourth. He opened the fifth by striking out Mantle for the second time. Then Maris fouled out.

Kicking his right leg high in the air, drawing his left arm far back toward second base, then surging forward and bringing his pitching arm through with all the weight and strength of his body behind it, Koufax was throwing fast balls as hard as any human

Sandy Koufax grimaces as he fires the ball.

has ever thrown them and his curve balls were breaking as though someone had rolled them off a table.

But at this point he faltered. He had gotten so many strikeouts so fast that he was trying to fire the ball past the batters instead of keeping them off balance. With two out in the fifth Elston Howard broke up the no-hitter by lining a single to right. Koufax shook his head angrily and tried to bust one past Joe Pepitone, who lined another single to right.

73

Sandy then worked on Clete Boyer, who drove the ball toward right center, but second baseman Dick Tracewski knocked the ball down, holding the lead runner on third. Now the bases were loaded. Hector Lopez pinch-hit for the pitcher. Bearing down, Koufax curved him several times, then struck him out on a fast ball.

It had been a long season and Koufax was tiring. He began to work more slowly and carefully now, refusing to break. In the sixth he walked two men, but Mantle and Maris hit pop-ups to end the inning. There were no strikeouts. In the seventh, Sandy struck out Howard and got Pepitone and Boyer on pop flies.

The Dodgers had picked up another run and Koufax entered the eighth with a 5–0 lead. After Phil Linz became Sandy's 13th strikeout victim, Kubek hit an infield single. Bobby Richardson fanned, then Tresh hit a fast ball, driving it into the lower deck in left field for two runs. Mantle walked, but then Sandy got Maris on an easy grounder for the third out.

In the ninth, with two out and a man on first, pinch-hitter Harry Bright came up. Koufax threw him nothing but fast balls, blasting the last one past him for a third strike and a new World Series record of 15 strikeouts in one game. As the Dodgers slapped him on the back and congratulated him, the fans gave him a huge ovation.

This was Koufax as he reached his peak, at the climax of his first big season. He had only three more years at the top of his profession before he retired because of an arthritic elbow. He did not have as many big years or as many total victories as many other pitchers, but he established records that may endure as long as baseball is played. He was as good in his prime as any pitcher has ever been.

Success did not come easily or quickly for Sandy. He grew to be a sensitive, moody person who would not reveal much of himself to the world.

He was born Sanford Koufax on December 30, 1935, and he grew up in Brooklyn. He was a quiet boy, not addicted to sports, and more interested in basketball than baseball. He joined a sandlot baseball team only to be with some friends. Beginning as a first baseman, he began to pitch only at the suggestion of a coach who was impressed by his throwing ability.

He accepted a basketball scholarship to the University of Cincinnati to study architecture. His pitching for the freshman team gained the attention of several major league clubs. During the summer, he was invited to try out with the then New York Giants and the Dodgers. He threw hard, but was wild. The Giants were not impressed, but the Dodgers offered him a $14,000 bonus to sign a contract with them.

After discussing it with his stepfather, he decided to take the offer. But for several years he continued to attend night school thinking that before long he'd be out of baseball and making his living as an architect. In spring training with the Dodgers in 1955, he was so wild he terrified batters who faced him. He was finally given a place to practice behind an old barracks where he could find his control without endangering the rest of the team.

The rules for bonus players required the Dodgers to keep Sandy in the majors. But the team was a pennant contender and was not eager to use a wild, uncertain pitcher. He pitched infrequently for the Dodgers in his first three seasons, winning nine and losing 10 games. In 1958 the Dodgers moved to Los Angeles and in his first three seasons there, Koufax worked only slightly more often, winning 28 games and losing 30.

Sandy was hard to hit, but he walked so

many men that a single hit was often enough to score runs and send Sandy out of the game. He wasn't working enough to master his art. At one point, he lost his temper to general manager Buzzy Bavasi, saying, "I want to pitch and I'm not getting a chance." Bavasi replied curtly, "How can we pitch you when you can't get the side out?" After six long seasons, Koufax was still an unimportant player.

Riding a bus during spring training in 1961, Sandy's roommate, catcher Norm Sherry, suggested to Sandy that if he threw less hard, he would still be faster than most pitchers and might have better control of his pitches. Sandy was skeptical, but agreed to try. From this suggestion in a casual conversation, greatness began to form. He pitched a no-hit game for seven innings against Minnesota in a late exhibition game and earned a chance to start a game early in the regular season. He allowed only six hits against Cincinnati and won a game during the first month of a season for the first time in his career. He was on his way.

Koufax won 18 and lost 13 that season and had 269 strikeouts. He began the next season brilliantly until he began to notice a numbness in his pitching hand. He had bruised the hand batting and he began to lose the feeling in his fingers. Soon blood-blisters began to form and the skin on the tip of his index finger dried up and began to flake off. His trouble was diagnosed as a rare circulatory disorder which could be controlled with medication. But Sandy was restricted to part-time duty and he compiled only a 14–7 record. He led the league with a 2.54 earned-run average, however—and would lead the league in this critical category for five straight seasons.

Although he was a husky 6-foot-2, 198-pounder, all his career Koufax was troubled by physical problems and often pitched in pain. Early in his career, he suffered a series of sore arms. When a teammate asked him why he was grimacing every time he pitched in one game, Sandy shrugged, "Making a face is nothing. I usually cry." In 1959, he suffered back pains which were

Koufax, hat knocked askew in the excitement, heads for the clubhouse after defeating the Yankees in the fourth and final game of the 1963 World Series.

not relieved until that winter when an operation removed a tumor on his left ribs.

Following the circulatory ailment of 1962, the heavily-muscled Koufax suffered a sore shoulder early in 1963, but after a two-week rest recovered to record a 25–5 mark with 306 strikeouts and a 1.88 ERA. In the World Series he won the first game. Then, after the Dodgers had won the next two he came back to win the fourth game, 2–1, on a two-hitter, completing a sweep of the mighty Yankees.

In 1964, his elbow troubled him but he had a 19–5 record and a remarkable 1.74 ERA. In 1965 he won 26 games and set a major league record with 382 strikeouts. With Don Drysdale, he helped pitch the Dodgers to another pennant. In the World Series he won two out of three games against Minnesota, including the crucial seventh game which gave the Dodgers another World Championship.

At times, Koufax was awesome. He twice tied Bob Feller's major league record by striking out 18 men in a game. He set a new major league mark by pitching four no-hitters; they came in consecutive years, 1962, 1963, 1964 and 1965. The last no-hitter was a perfect game in which Sandy pitched to only 27 batters.

In 1966, he won 27 games and lost only nine, led the league in shutouts with 11 and in strikeouts for the fourth time with 317 and in earned-run average for the fifth straight time with his best-ever mark, 1.73. Sadly, it was his last season.

Koufax had never been comfortable as a celebrity and a super-star. He resented intrusions on his privacy by press and public. Although he was making more than $100,-000 a year, he was a shy soul and disliked being in the spotlight. And by 1966 his elbow ached so horribly every time he pitched that he was in constant agony.

Koufax winces in pain between pitches. The pain in his elbow finally forced him to retire.

Prior to the next season, he ended the agony. Wistfully, almost tearfully, at the very pinnacle of his success, still able to pitch far more effectively than anyone else in the game, he announced his retirement. He was only 30 and might have pitched for many years to come.

Those who thrilled to his performances regretted the abrupt and startling end to a career that was far from its natural climax.

After 12 seasons in the major leagues, Koufax had a modest 165–87 record, but his eventual election to the Hall of Fame had been assured by the records he set in strike-outs and no-hit games and by a brief but spectacular succession of regular season and World Series achievements.

PETE MARAVICH

A capacity crowd of 11,000 jammed the Coliseum at Louisiana State University. The date was January 1970, and LSU fans had been waiting for this night for four years. Pistol Pete Maravich, their hero, needed just 40 points to become college basketball's all-time leading scorer. Although few players are capable of scoring so many points in one game, the crowd had no doubt that Pete would break the record. After all, he had averaged better than 44 points per game throughout his entire college career.

LSU took a big lead against Mississippi early in the game. By halftime Pete had scored 25 points. On the opening tipoff of the second half Pete got the ball and drove to the basket. He layed it up and scored, but crashed into the padded post that held up the backboard. The crowd hushed as Pete lay on the floor, then sighed in relief when he got up. He was stunned, but otherwise unhurt.

With 7:58 left in the game, Maravich banked in a 25-footer, giving him 39 points for the game. That shot also tied Pete's college total, 2,973, with the record set by the great Oscar Robertson of Cincinnati between 1957 and 1960. Now the LSU crowd began chanting, "One more, one more, one more!"

In the past, Pistol Pete seemed immune to pressure. But as the very special moment approached, Pete's nervousness showed. He missed on his next five shots. Finally, with 4:41 left, Pete moved to the right side of the court, found an opening in the Mississippi defense, and shot. Two points! Pistol Pete had the record.

Pete's teammates dashed toward him and hoisted him on their shoulders. Everyone in the Coliseum was on his feet cheering.

Socks drooping, hair flying, Maravich races downcourt with the ball.

Play was stopped for four minutes as Pete was given the game ball. The game hardly seemed worth continuing, but in the time left Pete scored 12 more points. Those points, plus the ones he would score in the remaining 12 regular-season games, probably would help make his record unbeatable for a long, long time.

After the Mississippi game, the interviews in the LSU dressing room went on for a good hour. The coach was in no hurry to shoo out the reporters, because the coach was also a very proud father. His name was Press Maravich.

"Who would have ever thought," said Press, "that that skinny little runt who grew up shooting baskets in Clemson would one day do something like this?"

Pete's success may have amazed his father, but Press had pointed Pete toward basketball from the beginning. Pete was born in Aliquippa, Pennsylvania, where his father was starting his coaching career. Earlier, Press had played pro ball. When Pete was old enough to hold a basketball, Press made sure he knew what to do with it. "I'd see Pete coming into the yard," said Press, "and I would run for the basketball and start shooting."

By the time Press moved to Clemson, South Carolina, to become head coach at Clemson University, Pete and the basketball were inseparable. He took it with him everywhere he went. At the movies Pete would sit on the aisle so he could practice dribbling. He would dribble while riding his bike, or even from a moving car. "Pete carried a basketball around like some kids carry a teddy bear," said his mother.

As an eighth-grader Pete made the starting line-up at Daniel High School. He was 5-foot-4 and weighed less than 100 pounds. In 1962 Press moved on to North Carolina State at Raleigh. Pete attended Needham Broughton High School, and averaged 32 points a game as a senior.

Throughout his high school career, coaches tried to change Pete's flamboyant style of play. He shot from all over the floor, taking all kinds of shots. His ball-handling was even more sensational. Pete dribbled behind his back or between his legs without breaking stride. He did tricks no one had ever seen before, and he refused to change.

"If I can get the ball to a man by passing it behind my back," he said, "what's the difference? That's my way. And the crowd loves it. Man, you can just feel them. When I hear the crowd roar, I swear I go wild, crazy! That's what I love most."

After graduation Pete went to prep school for a year. His father moved to Baton Rouge, Louisiana, to help build up the weak basketball program at LSU. Louisiana has always been football country. "Before Press came," one school official recalled, "our season ticket sale was about 40. I made my wife go to the game just so there would be one less empty seat."

Press' secret weapon in creating basketball interest was his son. When Pete enrolled at LSU in the fall of 1966, people could hardly wait to see him in action. Pete soon became one of the most colorful players in college basketball. At 6-foot-6 and 180 pounds, he was downright skinny. He had pipecleaner arms, floppy brown hair, and

Pete discusses strategy with his father, LSU coach Press Maravich.

Maravich goes up for a perfect jump shot against the University of Kentucky.

wore the same droopy gray socks that he had been wearing since high school. But Pete's agility with the ball is what made him a celebrity. "I move that ball around my body so fast," said Pete, "that sometimes even I don't know where it is. I mean I *move*!" The LSU Tigers created a warm-up drill which featured Pete in the middle with the ball, with three teammates weaving around him and the LSU band playing "Sweet Georgia Brown." The routine was called the "Globie Drill," after the Harlem Globetrotters.

In his first freshman game, before a

packed house, Pete scored 50 points. He also hit his teammates in the head with his passes, because they were not alert enough to catch them. After the game most of the fans left, not bothering to stay to watch the unimpressive varsity.

By the end of the season the varsity had won just three games, while the freshmen with Maravich had won all but one. The one loss occurred on the road against Tennessee. With LSU trailing, 75-73, and only eight seconds left, Pete stepped to the free-throw line. He made his first shot but missed the second. LSU lost by a point. Later that night, after the varsity game, Press got worried when he couldn't find his son. Pete had taken the loss so hard that he had walked the two miles from the fieldhouse to the motel.

As a sophomore, Pete helped the LSU Tigers achieve a respectable record of 14 wins and 12 losses. And he made believers out of the most skeptical coaches. Before LSU played Kentucky, famed Kentucky coach Adolph Rupp vowed he wouldn't resort to double- or triple-teaming to stop Maravich. But when the time came, Kentucky tried everything it could on Pistol Pete. Kentucky won, but Maravich scored 52 points. "This boy is as near the complete basketball player as you'll see anywhere," Rupp said after the game.

Pete averaged 43.8 points during his sophomore year and made all the All-America teams. But he did not make the '68 Olympic team. Naturally he was disappointed. "It was a once-in-a-lifetime thing and I missed it," he said.

During his junior year Pete made up for his disappointment by raising his scoring average to 44.2. By his final season he had become a legend. A fan wrote a folk song about him entitled "The Ballad of Pete Maravich." Broadcasts of LSU games were piped into more than a dozen states. There was a Pete Maravich fan club as far away as San Antonio, Texas, and letters poured in to Pete from all over the country.

Nevertheless, not everybody loved Pete and his father. Some felt that Press was "using" LSU by letting Pete pad his scoring average so that Pete could get a bigger pro contract. "For some reason," said Press, "they fail to understand that there's a difference between shooting and getting open for shots. Because of Pete's great quickness, his instinct, his ability to change directions on a dime, his sense—things he's developed by himself over a period of years—because of all these things our offense is naturally geared to his talents."

Critics also said that if Pete shot less, LSU might win more. Pete helped change that opinion by leading LSU to a 20–8 regular season record in his last season. That was the best LSU record in years, achieved against one of the roughest schedules in the country. LSU finished second in the Southeastern Conference and earned an invitation to the National Invitational Tournament. At the same time Pete again increased his season's average, finishing with 46.6.

By the time Pete had played his last regular season game he had scored 3,590 points. He attained his highest scoring—69 points—in a game against Alabama when he was a senior. And Pete had scored 50 or more points 26 times.

In early 1970, Pete signed to play pro ball with the Atlanta Hawks of the NBA. His contract called for more than $1½ million. Although his scoring had gotten him into the record books, many experts felt that Pete's greatest skill would be his passing. In any case, everyone agreed with one pro coach who said, "Pete's a master of the unexpected. He'll have those crowds in the palm of his hands."

JUAN MARICHAL

Juan Marichal had the most elaborate pitching style in modern baseball history. He reared far back, kicking his left foot up so high that it seemed to reach the sky, drawing his right hand so far back it sometimes scraped the ground. Then he uncoiled, exploding forward, hurling the ball at the batter. He continued his forward motion, staggering until he settled into a crouch, hopefully in time to field any ball that was hit back to him.

In June of 1963, he was warming up to pitch against Houston when teammate Willie McCovey walked past him. "I think I'll do something different this game," said Juan. "I'll change my windup and use the men-on-bases motion all the time. What do you say?"

At first, McCovey could say nothing. He just stared at Marichal. Then he said, "I think you're crazy. You just won five games in a row. You shut out Los Angeles in your last game. You've been pitching great your way. Why would you want to try another way?"

"Because Houston has been hitting me a little bit," Juan replied. "It looks like they are beginning to figure me out. So now it's time to give them something else to worry about."

Discarding his usual high-kicking, slingshot-throwing style, Marichal stood up straight, brought his hands together at the waist, then cocked his arm back, and fired. Confused, Houston batters hit only one solid drive—a fly to deep left field, where McCovey caught it. Marichal won a no-hit game.

Perhaps that one game typified Marichal, a pitcher who was able to do more things than any other hurler in the 1960s and was

Juan Marichal relaxes during his warm-up on the sidelines.

the dominant hurler of the decade. A fellow as sensitive as an artist, he worked like an artist on the mound.

Juan did his homework and always was prepared. He kept a "book" on rival batters. He avoided air-conditioning to protect his arm and constantly clipped his finger-nails "just so." He mastered new pitches and different deliveries. He usually used his elaborate windup, but he threw overhand, three-quarter-arm and side-arm, too. He threw fast balls and curve balls, change-ups,

81

Marichal shows his pitching form (above) while pitching a no-hit game against Houston in 1963. At right, he signs autographs for young fans in Cincinnati.

and even screwballs. He controlled everything magnificently. And he worked tirelessly. Over one five-year period he completed more than 90 per cent of his victories.

The great slugger Henry Aaron said, "His motion confuses you, his pitches elude you and he can throw all day through a six-inch hole. I've never seen anybody as good as he is."

Sandy Koufax, Marichal's main mound rival during the era, said, "It is his consistency that awes you. He pitches every fourth day and he pitches nine innings every game. He's as great as any I ever faced." Hall of Famer Carl Hubbell said, "He's the greatest I ever saw."

Juan Antonio Sanchez Marichal (pronounced "Mar–ee–CHAL") was born October 20, 1937, in a palm-bark shack in the poor village of Laguna Verde in the Dominican Republic, near the border of Haiti. His father died when Juan was 3. At 12,

Juan went swimming after a heavy meal, struggled in to shore suffering spasms and lost consciousness. A village doctor pronounced him dead. He was not. He lay in a coma six days, but recovered.

He grew up husky and strong. He worked in the fields, chopping sugar cane with a machete, and in the bay, diving for lobster. But he dreamed of being a great baseball pitcher. At first, he played shortstop on town teams, but his older brother, Garrido, a semi-pro performer, taught him how to pitch, and he became the best pitcher in his part of the country.

When he was 16, Juan's mother inherited 400 acres of farm land, which he worked for her. He loved to go skin-diving with his friends the Alou brothers, Felipe, Matty and Jesus, who later made baseball's major leagues, too. But most of his spare time, he played baseball.

One day he pitched a big game for the

United Fruit Company team in the port town of Manzanillo. His pitching talent was recognized and he was soon drafted into the Dominican Air Force, so that he could play for the service team which entertained the Republic's dictator, Trujillo. Juan was restless and unhappy in uniform, but his reputation spread until it reached the United States.

Marichal first came to the attention of Jack Schwarz, an official for the San Francisco Giants, through Horacio Martinez, a Dominican scout for the major leagues. Schwarz was interested but cautious. "If he wants too much money, forget it," Schwarz said. Marichal was offered $500 to sign. He took it. "It makes me shudder to know that we might have passed him up," Schwarz said later.

Marichal was 20 years old. He started out with Michigan City of the Midwest League in 1958 and pitched for Springfield in the Eastern League in 1959. In 1960 he pitched for Tacoma of the Pacific Coast League until the Giants called him up to San Francisco. Everywhere he went, his managers were amazed at how little they could teach him. He had such talent that he was overpowering right from the start. He won 40 games in three seasons in the minors.

As soon as he arrived in San Francisco, Bill Rigney, the manager of the Giants, asked him if he wanted to start a game right away. "Why not?" shrugged Marichal. In his first start, he shut out Philadelphia, permitting only one hit, a pinch single in the eighth inning. He won six of eight decisions that season, was 13–10 in 1961 and 18–11 in 1962. Through the remainder of the 1960s he failed to win 20 games or more only one season.

From 1963 through 1969, Marichal won 154 games and lost only 65, bringing his career record to 191–88 for a winning percentage of .685, one of the best in baseball history. The durable 5–11, 190-pounder averaged around 40 starts, 25 complete games and 300 innings a season, which were the best marks in baseball. His earned-run average was 2.6 per game. He struck out as many as 248 batters a season and walked as few as 62. No other pitcher of the 1960s was so effective for so long.

Yet Marichal never won the Most Valuable Player award in the National League, nor the Cy Young Award as the top pitcher. Nor did he receive the attention of a Koufax or a Dennis McLain. One reason may be that either Koufax or McLain had their greatest years when Marichal was having his best seasons. McLain and Koufax also played for teams that won pennants and World Series championships, while the Giants finished second most of the time.

Marichal may also have been underrated because of his background and personality. Handsome, with a chubby face, snub nose and curly black hair, Juan often seemed carefree in the company of fellow Latins. But he seemed moody, thin-skinned and explosive to other players, the press and the public.

In a game between the Giants and Dodgers in Candlestick Park in August of 1965, an ugly incident erupted between Marichal and Dodger catcher John Roseboro. The two teams were fighting for the pennant. Both teams had charged that "beanballs" had been thrown by opposing pitchers. Marichal had been accused of throwing too close to several Dodgers. He was at bat when Roseboro, returning the ball to the pitcher, threw close to Marichal's head. They exchanged words and Marichal hit Roseboro over the head with his bat. Players from both teams rushed to home plate and a riot nearly broke out.

"The ball ticked my right ear. I think Roseboro was trying to start a fight with me. He had on a face mask and chest protector, so I couldn't hit him with my hands. I lost my temper for a moment. I am sorry I hit him, but I do feel he asked for it," Marichal said later. He was fined $1,750 and suspended eight playing days by National League president Warren Giles. Many considered this insufficient punishment. Roseboro sued Marichal. Any chance Juan had to gain great popularity vanished forever.

Like many Latin players, he never has felt accepted or comfortable in the U. S. "My skin may be lighter, but the breaks I get are less than Negro players get both on and off the field," he has charged. He has resented being criticized for not coming through in the clutch when the Giants narrowly missed pennants. "I win and I win and it is not right I should get blamed," he complains. He feels that he had to fight the Giant management to make as much money as other stars, although he has earned as much as $125,000 a year.

At first, Juan was considered a traitor in the Dominican Republic because he deserted it to grow rich in the United States. In the spring of 1962, when there were political disturbances in the Dominican Republic, he hurried home to marry his 18-year-old sweetheart, Alma Rosa, and brought her back with him. However, he continued to maintain his permanent residence in his homeland and when he returned there each winter, the feelings of his countrymen softened. He came to be regarded by many as a hero.

He now has a 1,000-acre ranch there where he raises beans, rice and corn, keeps dairy and beef cattle, and breeds horses and fighting cocks. He spear-fishes in coral lagoons. He speaks longingly of the time when he will leave baseball and the United States for the life of a farmer in his own land.

ROGER MARIS

It was the final day of the 1961 season. The New York Yankees had already clinched the American League pennant, but seldom had there been such excitement in their old stadium in the Bronx. For today, Yankee outfielder Roger Maris had his last chance to beat Babe Ruth's home run record.

The flamboyant Ruth had hit 60 homers in 1927, playing a 154-game schedule. In more than 30 years his record had seldom been threatened. It had taken Maris 161 games in the longer modern season to hit 60, so technically he too had failed to break Ruth's record. But today he had a chance to hit his 61st—and become the only man in baseball history to do so.

"I'm not trying to replace Ruth," Maris had been saying. That might have been obvious, but many fans had turned against him as he closed in on the Babe's 60, the most venerated achievement in sports. Even Ruth's widow said she hoped Roger didn't surpass her late husband.

By the final day, however, the huge crowd in Yankee Stadium was solidly behind Maris. He was cheered loudly in batting practice. A young righthander, Tracy Stallard, was the Boston pitcher, and Maris was determined to take a lusty swat at any pitch that was close.

In the first inning, he was up with a runner on second. He drove a long fly ball to left field, but it was too high and not long enough, and it was caught. Maris, a lefthanded hitter, wished to himself that he had pulled it to right field, his power field.

Maris came up next in the fourth, with the score 0–0. The Stadium was strangely hushed, in expectation. Stallard, who vowed not to go down in history as the man who

In the last game of the 1961 season Roger Maris connects for his 61st home run, becoming the first man ever to hit so many in one year.

Maris became a celebrity almost overnight and regularly faced crowds of newsmen in the locker room after a game.

threw the pitch that Roger Maris hit for his 61st home run, fidgeted nervously on the mound. He threw a ball, then another. The crowd booed, rankling Stallard.

His third pitch was a fastball, over the plate, chest high. Maris was ready. He uncoiled and lashed a fierce line drive toward the short right field fence. It was a home run, the one that made him the most prolific slugger the game has seen.

He circled the bases in a daze, thinking only that it was his 61st—and that he couldn't be happier. After he crossed home plate his teammates congratulated and pummeled him, and held him up on the steps for the roaring crowd to salute. Maris had conquered the most dramatic record in baseball.

"All I know is I hit 61 homers this year," he said. "Nobody else ever did that in one year. I was just trying to do the best I could, and now I'm glad it's over."

The last two months of the season had been an ordeal for Roger. He was involved in a bristling race for the home run championship with teammate Mickey Mantle. Until the closing days of the season Yankee fans cheered for Mickey. They booed Maris for having the impertinence to challenge their long-time hero. He was scorned for threatening Ruth, scorned for threatening Mantle.

Maris and Mantle, sharing an apartment in New York, joked about the false reports that they were feuding, but Maris became more and more tense. Dozens of writers surrounded him before and after every game during September. He was hounded for autographs even in church. On the road he was forced to take his meals in drab hotel rooms because he would have been mobbed in a public dining room. Seldom has an athlete been subjected to more intense pressure. He became so nervous that his hair fell out in large chunks when he combed it.

Little in his background had prepared Maris for such a challenge. The son of a railroad employee, he grew up in the great outdoors, in Minnesota and North Dakota. In high school he showed more promise and interest in football and basketball than in baseball. He considered attending the University of Oklahoma to play football under the great Bud Wilkinson. But Maris decided to play professional baseball, and signed a modest bonus contract with the Cleveland organization.

His strong-mindedness quickly surfaced when Roger—only 18—insisted on playing in a Class C rather than a Class D league and further refused to accept any assignment other than to Fargo, his home town. Although it was a policy of the Cleveland system never to let a boy play in his home town, Maris won out. At Fargo in his first year as a pro he hit .325, with nine home runs.

The next season he was assigned to the Fargo roster again but refused to report, saying if he were not promoted to Class B ball he would quit. He was sent to Keokuk in the Class B Three-Eye League where Jo-Jo White was the manager.

White converted Maris from a spray hitter to a pull hitter, convincing him to make the most of his six feet and 197 pounds. Soon Maris was on his way as a home run producer: he hit 32 homers at Keokuk and still had a .315 average.

After two more years in the minors, Maris was brought up to the major leagues by the Indians in 1957. Maris began the season solidly and was mentioned often in early rookie-of-the-year talk. But he cracked a rib in breaking up a double play and his average fell from .300 to .235 by the end of the year. He hit 14 homers.

In 1958 the volatile Frank Lane became Cleveland's general manager, and clashed with Maris almost immediately when Maris declined to play winter ball, preferring to stay at home with his wife and children. In June, Maris was traded to Kansas City, where he batted .240 and hit 28 homers.

He began the 1959 season with Kansas City spectacularly, but he was slowed down by an attack of appendicitis and finished the year with a .273 average and 16 homers. Maris still had not approached his potential over a full season, and there were astute baseball men who were wondering aloud if he ever would. Maris had shown himself to be a reliable all-around ballplayer, a fine fielder and baserunner and even a clever bunter, but he was not a star.

Then in December of 1959 he was traded to the Yankees, and the deal turned around his career. Casey Stengel stationed him in left field and Maris unabashedly said he would prefer right, which is where he eventually played. In his first game as a Yankee, inspired by the club's tradition and pride, Maris ripped out two homers, a double and a single. During 1960 Maris hit 39 homers and was named the league's Most Valuable Player, winning the award by three points over Mantle.

"He's a little bit of a strange fellow, that Maris," said Stengel, "but one heck of a player."

Even so, there was slight reason to suggest that Maris was ready to launch an assault on Ruth's record. Maris was a good journeyman performer who had become the latest of many players who attained stardom after putting on a Yankee uniform. But 61 home runs? No one, including Maris, considered the possibility.

An inward-looking, unvarnished man, Maris was hard put to contend with the pressure of answering hundreds of questions by New York sports writers every day. After 1961 he never again felt at ease with some of them. In his anticlimactic later seasons with the Yankees, his public relations problems grew worse. He never came close to

Traded to the St. Louis Cardinals, Maris helped them win pennants in 1967 and 1968. Here he comes to bat in the Cardinal uniform.

his home run record again and injuries kept him below form, but he was never ignored by persistent writers.

It came as a relief to Maris to be traded in 1967 to the St. Louis Cardinals in the National League. In St. Louis he was not expected to hit 61 home runs again and did not face intense probing from the press. He could be a team player, one of the fellows— the Roger Maris he had been until 1961.

Maris' career closed on a solidly upbeat note. He was given a large amount of the credit for the Cardinals' pennants in 1967 and '68 and their World Series championship in '67. He led the Cardinals in game-winning hits that first season, and followed with an outstanding Series against Boston, hitting .385 and driving in seven runs. "My stroke hadn't been that good in a long while," he said.

His transformation from power hitter to team man was pointed up in the first game of the series. His first two times at bat, Maris drove in runners from third base by grounding the ball to the right side of the infield. "With less than two outs, you're supposed to get the man in any way you can," he said, sounding as pleased as if he had hit the ball over the fence. Once in the fourth game he hit the ball to the opposite field when Jose Santiago pitched him outside, and two more runs scored. "There's a lot more to this game than home runs," Maris said.

Nevertheless, he will be remembered for his 61 home runs. He retired after the 1968 season, never having reached the level of greatness a second time. But no one had seriously threatened Maris' record through the 1960s and it may be a good while before anyone does.

WILLIE MAYS

A rookie righthander pitching for San Diego, Mike Corkins, fought back the fear that any young pitcher would feel pitching to the Giants' Willie Mays. The Giants and San Diego were tied 2–2 in the seventh inning of a game that could affect San Francisco's chances in the 1969 pennant race.

Corkins fired the ball, and Willie's bat met it with an awesome crack. Mays had his 600th home run. In the history of major league baseball only one man had hit more —Babe Ruth collected 714 homers in his long career.

Characteristically, Mays' home run had done more than set a record—it had won an important game. In the previous year, although nearing the end of his career, Willie had led the major leagues in game-winning hits. "I like pressure," he said. "I like to come to bat when I really have to get a hit."

Mays was not interested in retrieving the ball he had hit for his 600th home run. At first it was kept by a 15-year-old fan who had caught it. Later it was sent to baseball's Hall of Fame, which is more interested in souvenirs than Willie Mays is. "I don't care that much about records," he said. "I care about winning games. It was more of a thrill winning the game with a home run than getting a record."

No one doubts that Willie eventually will follow the ball into the Hall of Fame. His election may be delayed, however, since he must be retired for five years before he is eligible. Mantle and Koufax and other superstars of Willie's generation had retired and are gone, but as the 1970s began Willie was still active after 20 years as a pro.

Can he hit as many home runs as Ruth? "I doubt it," he says, "but I'm going to hit a few more. With expansion, there are more home runs. If I can stay healthy another four or five years I might have a chance. I get plenty of rest and don't have any bad habits, and I feel good. Sometimes it's work, but mostly I still enjoy the game."

In the late 1960s, Willie had injuries and occasional dizzy spells to slow him down. But even they did not suppress Willie's remarkable enthusiasm for baseball. In fact, some of the injuries may have been caused by his perpetual go-go-go attitude. Running out from under his cap, grabbing a screaming line drive with his bare hand, sliding recklessly into a base—this is Willie Mays, past and present.

Willie grew up in Alabama, a poor boy who was unsure of himself, but from the very beginning he had a special kind of enthusiasm. In 1950, his first year in organized ball, he hit .353 for the Giants' farm club at Trenton, and impressed the parent club with his great natural moves. After 35 games in 1951, Willie was hitting .477 at Minneapolis in the American Association, and Giant manager Leo Durocher called him to the major leagues. Then followed the worst period of Willie's career.

In his first three games as a big leaguer he did not get a hit. In the fourth game he pounded a home run, but then he went 0-for-13. It was a bad week, and Willie seemed ready to give up. He told Durocher that he wasn't good enough for the National League, and asked Durocher to send him back to Minneapolis. "Don't be silly," Durocher said, throwing an arm around Mays' shoulders. "You're staying right here, so quit worrying about it. You'll be fine."

Mays banged out two hits the next day, gained confidence as the season wore on,

and eventually hit .274. He helped the Giants to a memorable drive for the pennant. The Giants, who then were in New York, trailed their crosstown rivals, the Brooklyn Dodgers, by 13½ games in mid-August. At the end of the regular season the two teams were tied. The Giants won the pennant in the ninth inning of the third playoff game with the Dodgers.

"Mays carried us on his back the second half of the season," said Durocher. With Durocher's help, Mays had made the Giants for good at the age of 20.

Before his career really got started, though, Mays spent two years in the Army. He returned for the 1954 season, and began to build his reputation as a superstar. He led the league with an average of .345, and helped the Giants to another pennant and a sweep of the World Series. Willie was named Most Valuable Player in the league.

The 1954 season was the first of 10 seasons in which he would drive in more than 100 runs, the first of six in which he would hit at least 40 home runs, and the first of 12

in a row in which he would score at least 100 runs. Soon he was being compared to his boyhood hero, Joe DiMaggio, who had retired in Mays' rookie year.

Willie's hitting was only part of the story. There is no accurate count of the seemingly impossible catches he made in center field, of the brilliant throws he made or of the bases he gained with his daring base-running. Willie would make dozens of dramatic plays, but none more spectacular than his catch in the 1954 Series against Cleveland. In the eighth inning of the first game it was 2–2. The Indians' Vic Wertz hit a long fly ball to center field, far over Mays' head, with two men on base.

Mays pivoted and raced toward the 460-foot sign for what seemed like five minutes, never looking back. At the last possible instant, his back still to the infield, he stretched out his glove hand as far as he could reach—and speared the ball on the dead run. Then he stopped, whirled, and whipped a long throw in to prevent a runner from scoring. It was quite possibly the most

Willie Mays cocks the bat (left), strides into the ball (center), and turns (right) in time to see it disappear into the stands—a foul ball.

impressive fielding play in World Series history.

There were other great days. One July day in 1961, Mays, not yet known as a home run producer, homered four times against the Braves, twice off Lew Burdette. He referred to it as "the greatest day I ever had."

In the waning days of the 1962 season, the Giants, who had moved to San Francisco, were fighting the Dodgers, who were now in Los Angeles, for the pennant. Willie's 47th home run of the regular season won the game that assured San Francisco of a tie with the Dodgers. In the first play-off game, Mays homered twice as the Giants won. In the third and decisive game, he singled to keep a ninth-inning rally going and the Giants finally won the game and the pennant.

In September of 1965, Willie ripped his 500th home run, against Houston in the Astrodome. He had followed through with only his left hand on the bat, leading a veteran baseball man to say increduously: "He

just hit a tape-measure homer with one hand!"

Willie closed the decade strongly, although not with the dominating statistics of his younger years. From 1966 through 1969 his batting average hovered around .280 and he chipped away at Ruth's career home run record. The Giants finished second all four years.

Willie lost some of his dash on the field but he also developed into the Giants' team leader, as well as a perennial All-Star. He worked extra hours developing the Giants' new prodigies, relying mainly on the force of example. "You don't want to show anybody up—you want to show him how to improve," Willie put it succinctly. He also counseled players on outside involvements. He consulted frequently with his manager on tactics and squad morale.

In 1965 during a heated Giant-Dodger game, Juan Marichal of the Giants, overcome by emotion, slammed catcher Johnny Roseboro of the Dodgers in the head with a bat, and a near-riot followed. Mays rushed in from the outfield and was the principal peacemaker. He raced from one tangled knot of irate players to another, pulling them apart and urging order before someone was seriously injured. "He had the coolest head of anybody out there," said a Dodger coach.

Mays' cool head and extensive major-league experience made him a good prospect for a managing job when his playing days end. There was also a chance that he would become the first black manager in the major leagues. He would like to be the man to break that barrier, not for racial reasons, which he always has downplayed, but because he wants to stay in the game and believes he is capable.

"You can't play in the major leagues as long as I will and not learn a lot about managing," he says.

In the meantime, Willie continued on the playing field in quest of Ruth's home run record and approached his 3,000th hit. He continued to draw thousands of additional fans every time he played. San Francisco fans, who had been slow to warm to Willie's multi-faceted ability, finally accepted him. He was even more popular on the road than at home. In New York, when he visited Shea Stadium to play against the Mets, he was welcomed like royalty.

The fans there have not forgotten the irrepressible Willie Mays who played for the Giants when they were in New York and who played stickball in the streets in his spare time. Even today it wouldn't be surprising to find Willie on a Harlem street, his jacket off, playing stickball with the same zest and spirit he brought to the major leagues.

Mays (right) relaxes in the locker room with his teammate, pitcher Juan Marichal.

DENNY McLAIN

Denny McLain keeps his eye on the target as he rocks back to throw.

Denny McLain of the Detroit Tigers was in a tight spot. The Boston Red Sox were one run behind and had men on second and third. Carl Yastrzemski, the defending American League batting champion, was at bat. McLain fired a fastball high and inside. Yaz swung and missed. McLain fired the second pitch, also a high inside fastball. Again Yaz swung and missed.

At this point most pitchers would have wasted a pitch or two, hoping to make the hitter swing at a bad pitch. But Denny

didn't believe in letting up. "I throw the pitch I want," McLain said, "and I dare the batter to try and hit it."

So Denny fired another fastball across the plate to Yaz. This time the Boston slugger fouled it off. Still Denny wouldn't back off. Three more times he fired fastballs for strikes, and three more times Yaz fouled them off. Finally, on the seventh straight fastball, Yaz swung mightily and missed. He walked unhappily back to the dugout, one of Denny McLain's 280 strikeout victims in 1968.

Denny's fastball wasn't his only strikeout pitch. The 6-foot, 190-pound right-hander threw a good curve, a teasing changeup and a slider. He could deliver each of his pitches overhand, sidearm, or three-quarter. Finally, he had pinpoint control.

Tiger pitching coach Johnny Sain, himself a great pitcher in the 1940s, was amazed. "For his age Denny has done better than any other pitcher I've ever known."

McLain was only 24 years old in 1968. Sandy Koufax was 27 when he first won 20 games in a season and Whitey Ford was 32. But for Denny, 20 wins already was old stuff. He had won that many in 1966, when he was 22. By 1968, he was ready for even greater things.

Denny won his 20th victory of 1968 in late July. People began wondering if he could win 30 before the end of the season. No one had won 30 games since 1934. Confident and cool as always, Denny continued to give up an average of less than six hits and two runs a game. Each victory for McLain brought him closer to the magic 30 games and brought the Tigers closer to the pennant. Detroit hadn't won one in 23 years.

McLain and teammate Al Kaline rush out to the field as the winning Detroit run scores, giving McLain his 30th win of the 1968 season.

With more than two weeks to go in the season the Tigers clinched the pennant, and a week later Denny won his 29th. His first try for Number 30 would come against the Oakland Athletics, in Detroit.

In the first three innings against Oakland, Denny was overpowering. He gave up only a single. In the fourth inning, however, Reggie Jackson hit a home run. In the sixth he hit another homer, putting the A's ahead, 4-3.

The Tigers still trailed by that one run when they came to bat in the bottom of the ninth. Denny was scheduled to bat first, but manager Mayo Smith decided to put in a pinch-hitter. Denny's pitching for the day was over. He had given up just six hits and had struck out ten.

If Denny was to win No. 30 in this game, the Tigers had to score two runs in the ninth. The pinch-hitter, Al Kaline, walked. He went to third on a single by Mickey Stanley and sprawled into home on a grounder to first, tying the score 4–4. McLain paced nervously up and down in the dugout.

There was only one out and Willie Horton was up. The A's outfielders moved in ready to make a play at the plate to prevent the winning run. But Horton slugged a pitch over the left fielder's head. Stanley came home from third. The Tigers had won, 5-4. Denny McLain and his teammates rushed onto the field to congratulate Horton. The capacity crowd in Tiger Stadium cheered wildly. A pitcher had just won 30 games for the first time in 34 years.

Denny McLain was born in Chicago on March 29, 1944. Early in his life he developed a love for playing baseball and for playing the organ. He gained both of those interests from his father. His dad was an insurance adjustor. But he had once been a semipro shortstop and he earned extra money giving organ lessons.

As a youngster Denny couldn't decide which he liked better, the organ or baseball, so he tried to give equal time to both. Once he was playing a game in the park across the street from his house. Suddenly he called time out and ran into the house to play a couple of songs, making sure he played loud enough to be heard across the street. "I knew a lot of people who thought it was a sissified thing to do," Denny has said about his organ playing, "and I beat up some of the guys who said it out loud."

Denny's interest in baseball finally won out over his interest in music. His big ambition was to play in the major leagues. In high school he played in five or six leagues at one time, and he was the star pitcher on each team.

When he was 15 he gained a friend and lost another. During a Babe Ruth League game, he struck out and angrily threw his bat into the stands. It hit a pretty dark-haired girl on the leg. Her name was Sharyn Boudreau, the daughter of the former Cleveland Indian star, Lou Boudreau. Sharyn would one day become Denny's wife. That same year, Denny's father died. On his way to see Denny pitch, he collapsed and died of a heart attack. He was only 36.

Denny graduated from high school in 1962 and received a $17,000 bonus to sign with the Chicago White Sox. They sent him to their minor league team in Harlan, Kentucky, where he pitched a no-hitter in his first pro game. But a few days later he left the club and went home. Denny was a big-city boy and didn't like what he considered a "hick town."

The White Sox then sent him to Clinton, Iowa, and again Denny didn't care for the place. He pitched a game, won it, and then went home. This time, the White Sox ordered him to return to the team or give up baseball. He gave in, returned to Clinton and paid a $100 fine. But he soon jumped the club a second and a third time. The second time he was fined $200 and the third time $300. "Boy, was I rotten," he said later. "But when they hit me with that $300 buckeroo, I started to get the message."

The White Sox were tired of his antics, however. The next spring they gave up on him and allowed Detroit to claim him for the $8,000 waiver price. After playing for two Tiger farm teams, Denny came up to the major leagues late in the 1963 season. His first major-league game was against the White Sox, and Denny won, 4–3. He was still only 19.

In 1964 Denny was hindered by back trouble. By mid-1965 he was in top form again. In June he tied a league record by striking out seven batters in a row. He went on to win eight games in a row and finished with a 16-6 record.

McLain won 20 games in 1966. The next year he won 17 games and lost 16. During that year Denny seemed to make more enemies than friends. He angered his teammates by calling the Tigers a "country-club ball team," and he angered the fans in Detroit by calling them "the worst anywhere." Worst of all, during September when the Tigers were fighting for the pennant, Denny didn't win a single game.

Denny spent the last two weeks out of the lineup, nursing two dislocated toes. He came back to pitch the last game of the season. If the Tigers could win it, they would tie the Red Sox and force a play-off. But Denny was knocked out of the game and the Tigers lost the game and the pennant. "When I left that game, it was the first time in a long time that I remember tears coming to my eyes," Denny said. "I felt so bad about letting those guys down."

Denny made it up to the team in 1968. He finished the regular season with a 31-6 record and a remarkable 1.96 earned-run average. And the Tigers won the pennant easily.

McLain wasn't as effective in the World Series as he had been during the regular season. He lost the first and fourth games to the St. Louis Cardinals, putting the Tigers in the hole, 3 games to 1. But Detroit won the fifth game and Denny redeemed himself with a 13–1 victory in the sixth game. The Tigers won the seventh game and became champions of the world.

Denny was voted Most Valuable Player in the American League in 1968. He was the first pitcher in the league ever to win the award on a unanimous vote. His honors and achievements left people wondering what Denny could do for an encore. They

With an Angel runner on second, McLain confers with Detroit catcher Bill Freehan.

got their answer in the last half of the '69 season.

The Tigers had fallen far behind the Baltimore Orioles. Denny was fighting a severe case of tendonitis in his right shoulder and needed cortisone shots even to keep pitching. Although he was in pain and the Tigers were out of contention for the pennant, Denny refused to miss a turn. He tied for the major-league lead in innings pitched with 325. He finished with a 24–9 record, including nine shutouts. That gave him a career record of 114 wins and 57 losses,

making him one of the youngest pitchers ever to win 100 or more games.

In early 1970, Denny was accused of associating with gamblers. After investigation of the charges, the commissioner of baseball suspended McLain for the first half of the 1970 season. But his achievements were already spectacular and his potential was still great. As manager Mayo Smith of the Tigers has said, "You can't say this fellow is a fluke. He's brash enough, confident enough and young enough to be one of the great ones."

JOE NAMATH

"Third down and four yards to go," said an old quarterback, watching the Super Bowl game from high in the stands. "There are no tougher words a quarterback can hear. Should you run for it? Or should you pass for it? The good quarterbacks make those third-and-fours, the bad ones don't."

Down on the football field Joe Namath stared, hands on hips, at the Baltimore Colt defense. This was the second quarter of the Super Bowl game on January 12, 1969, the Colts against the New York Jets. The Jets, from the young American Football League, were 17-point underdogs against this powerful Colt team from the older National Football League.

The score was 0–0, the ball on the Colt 48, third down and four to go. On the snap Namath darted back, turned and angled a pass toward flanker George Sauer on the right side. Sauer grabbed the ball on the 34 for the first down. The good quarterbacks make them, the bad ones don't.

A minute later Joe and the Jets were standing on the Colt 4. He handed off to fullback Matt Snell who plunged into the end zone for a touchdown. For the first time, an AFL team led in the Super Bowl, 7–0.

Two hours later the Jets were still leading, 16–7. A pistol shot signaled the end of the game and Joe Namath and the Jets rushed, exultant, off the field, the first AFL team to win in the Super Bowl.

For Joe Willie Namath, the quarterback with the two bad knees, the triumph was doubly satisfying. Years earlier, when he had signed a $400,000 contract to play for the Jets, he told someone: "I've played in only four losing games in five years of high school and college football. That's because

Joe Namath and the Jets congratulate each other after defeating the Baltimore Colts in the 1969 Super Bowl.

I've been associated with good people, with winners. I think that's one reason why the Jets wanted me. Well, I intend to be associated with winners this year and for years after."

Now he was with a winner again. His triumph was also satisfying because Joe had predicted it would happen. "We will beat the Colts," he told reporters over and over again before the Super Bowl. Some people had laughed, but Joe's word was good.

The triumph pushed Joe Namath to the top of the list of great quarterbacks. Joe Namath, the swinger, had replaced Bart Starr and Johnny Unitas, the quiet homebodies, as the most admired active quarterback in football.

Namath has spotted his receiver and throws the ball on-target.

Joe Namath was a symbol of a new generation. He had shaggy hair and long sideburns, and a cocky attitude toward the established way of doing things. He challenged the rules, staying out late, and enjoying the bubbly side of life. But he could be deadly serious and as efficient as a machine on a football field.

Joe was a born passer. Opposing linemen claimed he could run back into a pocket faster than any other quarterback. He released the ball with the quickness of a snake striking, and his passes were deadly accurate. In one game two linemen hit him in the chest. Toppling backward, he threw the ball 45 yards into the hands of a receiver waiting in the end zone.

Not surprisingly, he had large hands that were as quick as a pickpocket's. He often entertained friends with slick sleight-of-hand card tricks.

He was equally slick at putting people on. One day at a practice session Jet coach Weeb Ewbank hollered, "You can't throw the ball down the middle on that play, Joe. There's a linebacker there."

"What linebacker, Weeb?" Joe asked seriously. "There's something wrong with your eyes. There's no linebacker there."

The stumpy Weeb stood on his tiptoes to look for the linebacker who had moved out of the play. "I was sure I saw a linebacker . . ." he said.

Then Joe began to laugh and Weeb knew he had become the latest victim of the Namath put-on.

In the light-hearted personality of Broadway Joe, there was also a more serious facet. He played from one game to the next, never knowing when his bad knees might collapse under him and end his career. Because of this uncertainty he seemed eager to enjoy his fame today because tomorrow it might be gone.

"I wonder how anyone can plan ahead—one month, two months ahead—when this could be your last day, your last hour," he once told a reporter. "Who knows where I will be two months from now? How can you know?"

Even at the peak of his fame, he never forgot the little town of Beaver Falls in western Pennsylvania, where he was born on May 31, 1943, the son of a steel worker. After his Super Bowl victory he went back to Beaver Falls for a celebration, spending hours talking with boyhood pals who worked in the town's steel mills.

Once, when Joe was a boy, his father had taken him to visit a mill. The boy had gasped at the heat of the furnaces and the ear-ringing clangor of the mill. He resolved that he would never work in a mill.

As a boy, he lived for sports. Though he was only five feet tall and 115 pounds in junior high school, he quarterbacked the school football team. "You could see that Joe had inborn talent," his high school coach, Larry Bruno, once said. "He could pick up a ping-pong paddle or a golf club and do well the first time."

By his senior year in high school Joe had grown to a powerful 6-foot-1 and 175 pounds. Wearing number 19, the number of his idol, Johnny Unitas, Joe guided little Beaver Falls High to an undefeated season. That winter he was the star on the basketball team. In one game, with Beaver Falls trailing by a point, he held the ball until the game's last second. Then he let fly a 30-foot shot. With the ball still in the air, he shot up two fingers as a victory sign. The ball swished through the nets for the two points that won the game.

He was just as confident with a baseball bat in his hand. He hit so well that Kansas City offered him a $15,000 bonus to sign. Joe and his father decided he should get a college education. Sorting through dozens of scholarship offers, he picked the University of Maryland but, never much for studying, he failed the entrance examination. In the fall of 1961 he entered the University of Alabama.

At Alabama he soon acquired a southern drawl and—in his sophomore year—the job of No. 1 quarterback for Alabama. In his first game, against Georgia, he completed 10 of 14 passes as Alabama won, 35–0. The Crimson Tide went on to win all but one game. On New Year's Day, 1963, they played Oklahoma in the Orange Bowl. With President John F. Kennedy watching, Joe completed 9 of 17 passes and Alabama won, 17–0.

The Tide lost only one game in 1963 and was invited to the Sugar Bowl. Joe didn't play in the Bowl: he had been suspended from the team for violating a training rule. Angry at himself, Joe apologized to his coach and promised he'd be fit for the 1964 season.

He was. Alabama won three straight victories at the start of the season. In the fourth game, against North Carolina State, Namath rolled to his right to pass and swerved to avoid a tackler. Suddenly his right leg collapsed under him. He limped off the field. Doctors said he had twisted cartilage in his knee.

Though limping and in pain, Namath went on playing for Alabama. The Tide finished the season unbeaten and was ranked No. 1 in the nation in several polls. For the third straight year the team went to a bowl game, this time to the Orange Bowl to play Texas.

Several days before the game, Joe's knee collapsed under him a second time. He wasn't supposed to play but he did, leading the Tide on a last-minute touchdown drive that fell short inches from the goal line.

After a jolting tackle, Joe gets up slowly. Even good pass blocking and a fast release are not always enough to stop tough defensive teams.

Texas won 21–17. Namath, limping and in pain, had completed 18 of 27 passes for two touchdowns. He was named the game's Most Valuable Player.

After finishing at Alabama, Joe signed with the Jets in the young American Football League. Many football fans thought he was making a mistake by signing with a poor team in a league they considered second-best. But he received a guarantee of $400,000 and he knew he would have a chance to play regularly. The AFL was counting on Joe to help disprove the charge that the league was second-best.

Early in 1965 before his first season with the Jets, doctors operated on Joe's right knee to repair the damaged cartilage. Although he played all season with a brace on the knee that hobbled him, he was named the league's Rookie of the Year.

In 1966 Namath's left knee began to give him trouble. A tendon in the knee had become inflamed because Joe was running in an abnormal way to favor the right knee.

Yet he performed brilliantly and was picked as quarterback on the AFL's second All-Star team. The Jets finished with a 7–7 record, their best ever.

After the 1966 season surgeons operated again on the right knee, trying to brace it up. In spite of operations, that scarred knee would pain and hobble Joe Namath for the rest of his career. But he came back in 1967 to become the first quarterback in pro football to gain more than 4,000 yards passing in one season. And the Jets were contenders for the AFL championship with an 8–5–1 record.

Then came the 1968 season. The Jets took the AFL championship and beat the Colts in the Super Bowl. The season brought the AFL recognition as an equal with the older NFL and brought Namath recognition as pro football's best quarterback. "If he had two good knees," San Diego quarterback John Hadl once said, "it wouldn't be fair to the rest of us to try to play on the same field with Joe Namath."

JACK NICKLAUS

Jack Nicklaus, Arnold Palmer and Billy Casper—golf's three top money-winners—were locked together in a tight struggle. Within a stroke or two of each other, they came to the final five holes of the 1967 Bing Crosby Open.

Palmer, who liked to gamble, decided to take a risk on his drive from the 14th tee. He pointed to two tall oak trees guarding the green 260 yards away. "I'm going over them," he said to his caddie.

He hit a soaring drive that struck a tree with a loud clunk. His second shot hit the tree again and ricocheted out of bounds. Those two bad shots knocked Palmer out of contention.

The methodical-hitting and smooth-putting Casper hit a drive straight down the middle of the 14th fairway. But the ball ran into a hole. Although Casper punched the ball out of the hole, it flew wide of the green. An angry Casper bogied the hole.

Cool and collected, Jack Nicklaus whacked his drive far down the fairway, then dropped his second shot onto the green and parred the hole. He knocked in birdie putts on three of the next four holes to win the tournament with a 284—five strokes ahead of Casper, seven strokes ahead of Palmer. "Head-to-head competition like this is pure fun," Jack said in his chirpy voice. "It's the kind of golf I enjoy the most."

Casper, Palmer and Nicklaus, along with Gary Player, were the champions of golf during the Sixties. Of the four, Nicklaus was the leading money-winner. Nobody in the history of golf won money at a faster clip than "Ohio Fats," as the pros called Jack. From 1962, his rookie season, through 1969 he averaged well over $100,-

Jack Nicklaus follows the flight of an iron shot during the 1967 British Open.

000 a year; Palmer, by contrast, earned an average of around $75,000 a year.

Altogether Nicklaus earned more than $800,000 in his first eight years of tournament golf. At the end of the decade only Palmer and Casper, who had played more seasons, had earned more. Nicklaus hoped to catch both of them and become golf's greatest all-time money-winner.

Jack Nicklaus caught fame by the tail with dramatic suddenness. During 1962, while attending college, he defeated Palmer to win the U. S. Open. He was only 22 years old. Palmer was 25 when he won his first tournament and Ben Hogan was 35.

Nicklaus went on to win all the major tournaments: the 1963 Masters, the 1963 PGA, the 1964 Tournament of Champions, the 1965 Masters, the 1966 Masters and British Open, and the 1967 U. S. Open.

Nicklaus' success surprised some pro golfers. "He has got so much weight around his gut," Sam Snead once said, "it has got to hurt his swing." Five feet 11 inches tall, Nicklaus has weighed as much as 235, his shirts ballooning over his beltline. Several years ago, after months of strict dieting and strenuous exercise, Nicklaus lost almost 30 pounds. He showed up for the Doral Tournament in Miami looking slimmer than he had ever been as a pro.

"Hey, Fats," Sam Snead said when he saw Nicklaus, "you've lost weight. How much do you weigh now?"

"Only two hundred and ten," Nicklaus said.

Arnold Palmer overheard. "Two hundred and ten!" he said, laughing. "Imagine that. Why he's getting to be a skinny man."

When not dieting, Jack's appetite was prodigious. At a dinner one night in New Orleans, Jack devoured 50 small lobsters, a plate of crab legs, a shrimp cocktail, a thick steak and a platter of popovers.

"I would have been hungrier," he said, his blue eyes flashing amusement, "but I had four-dozen oysters a little while ago and they took away some of my appetite."

However, Nicklaus' size and marvelous coordination helped to make him one of the longest hitters among the pros. "Maybe one or two percent of the pros can outdrive Jack," George Bayer, himself a long-ball hitter, once said. "But Jack is the longest accurate hitter in golf."

In one tournament Jack was playing a 548-yard par-5 hole. Most pros would have reached the green in three shots: a 250-yard drive with a wood, a 220-yard wood shot short of the green, and an 80-yard pitch to the green with a short iron. Nicklaus slammed a 350-yard drive, then pulled a seven-iron out of his bag and whistled the ball some 200 yards onto the green. The ball stopped 15 feet from the cup, giving him a chance for an eagle on the hole.

Jack has been hitting those long drives ever since he was a boy back in Columbus, Ohio, where he was born on January 21, 1940. When Jack was ten his father, who owned a chain of drug stores, injured an ankle. To strengthen it, he began to play golf, and took Jack along. After two days of watching, Jack wanted to play. The first time Jack played, he shot a 51 for nine holes, swinging cut-down clubs given to him by his father.

"By the time Jack was twelve I couldn't handle him any more on a golf course," his father once said. "I remember one day I hit as good a drive as I could, maybe 260 yards. I told Jack, 'If you outhit that one, I'll buy you a Cadillac convertible.' He hit the ball 20 or 30 yards past mine and I never outdrove him again."

When Jack finished high school he entered Ohio State to study business. By that time he had a room-full of trophies. He had

During his playoff round with Arnold Palmer in the 1962 U.S. Open, Nicklaus grits his teeth as his putt on the 13th green rolls wide of the cup. His luck improved, though, and he beat Palmer by two strokes.

won the Ohio Open at 16, the National Jaycee Tournament at 17, and at 19 the U. S. Amateur Championship. In 1959 he went to Scotland with the U. S. Walker Cup team and won both his matches as the U. S. team beat the British team, 9–3.

In the nationally televised 1960 U. S. Open, the 20-year-old Jack caught the eyes of millions as he battled Palmer down to the final hole. He finished second, only two strokes behind Arnie. It was the highest finish for an amateur since the 1933 Open.

When Jack won the 1961 U. S. Amateur, friends urged him to turn pro. He did so at the start of the 1962 tournament season and surprised the golf world by finishing in a tie with Palmer after 72 holes of the U. S. Open at Oakmont, Pennsylvania. In the playoff round, the collegian matched Palmer stroke for stroke for most of the first 12 holes. Palmer, the world's most famous golfer, had an army of thousands cheering for him. Nevertheless, Nicklaus remained calm.

With six holes to play Jack trailed Palmer by one shot. Nicklaus knocked in a putt to par the 13th. Palmer bogied a hole, and they were even. Palmer bogied another hole and Nicklaus pulled ahead to win the Open. At 22 he was the youngest U. S. Open champion in 39 years.

Competing with the colorful Palmer, Jack never received the acclaim his performance deserved. Some golf fans even taunted him. Once at Augusta, during a playoff for the 1966 Masters, Nicklaus hit a shot that streaked toward a pond. "Get into the water, Fat Jack," yelled a spectator, and many people laughed.

But Nicklaus won the respect of the galleries at the 1967 U. S. Open. On the 18th hole he hit a 1-iron to within 22 feet of the cup. Ahead by four strokes, he could have cozied the ball into the hole with two or three careful strokes. Instead he boldly went

After breaking Ben Hogan's U.S. Open record in 1967, Nicklaus shakes hands with Arnold Palmer on the 18th green.

for the cup and sank the putt to finish with a 275, one stroke under Hogan's old Open record.

Nicklaus frequently hopped off the tournament trail, flying in his own plane to his palatial home near West Palm Beach, Florida, to spend time with his wife and children and to fish. The house sat on the edge of a golf course, only a few hundred feet from a dock where Jack's big cabin cruiser was tied up. His idea of a perfect afternoon was to buzz out into the ocean and fish.

"I love to fish," he said. "When I take time out from the tour, I come home and go on a fishing trip. I don't even think about golf. When I go back to the tournaments, I feel fresh and relaxed. I expect to be fishing and playing golf for a long, long time."

Fishing and golfing and, of course, winning.

BOBBY ORR

As Bobby Orr walked toward the locker room, he realized he had never been more scared. He was about to join his new teammates, the Boston Bruins, and he knew he was on the spot. Here he was, just 18 years old, without a minute's experience in pro hockey.

People had predicted that he would become a superstar and he had received a two-year contract for $65,000. That was more money than any of the Bruins were making, even though many of them had been in the National Hockey League for years. Bobby didn't know how his teammates would react to all this, but he guessed that they would test him pretty quickly to find out what he was made of.

When Bobby entered the locker room, the Bruins already were there. Spread out in front of them was a blanket. "Lay down on it," one of them said. "It's a magic blanket."

Bobby could tell by the looks on the veterans' faces that he didn't have any choice. But he also was curious, and wondered if there was anything magic about the blanket. So he lay down on it.

Suddenly, the Bruins jumped him. One of them took out a safety razor and began shaving Bobby—without water or shaving cream. The player scraped the razor across Bobby's crewcut, his face, up and down his body. When they finished, Bobby was nicked with dozens of cuts.

Bobby was in pain, but he knew he didn't dare cry out. This was the Bruins' test—to see if the boyish-looking Orr could take physical punishment like a man. As a Bruin player said afterward, "It was better that he got the 'business' from us first, because everybody and his brother [on the other teams] was sitting in the wings just waiting to get a piece of him."

Orr had proved to his teammates that he could take it, and he began proving it to opponents in the 1966 season. They came at him with elbows, fists and sticks. They speared him, tripped him, and jabbed him in the ribs. But Bobby took it, and he gave it right back. Once, when Reggie Fleming, the notorious "bad boy" of the New York Rangers, jammed his stick into Orr's stomach, Bobby dumped him with a vicious bodycheck.

Rough tactics couldn't slow Bobby down, and neither could anything else. He was every bit as talented as it was predicted he would be. In fact, he was better. Within two seasons he had emerged as the best defenseman in the game, and within four years he was unquestionably the best complete player as well. In the 1969–70 season he led the NHL in scoring, an incredible and unprecedented feat for a defenseman. "Orr is almost unbelievable," Bruin general manager Milt Schmidt said. "He can do everything. We have to find out what he can't do."

Bobby's two greatest assets were his speed and power. He probably was the swiftest skater in the league, and able to shift gears at will. "He has 18 speeds of fast," said a teammate. As for Bobby's strength, it was deceptive. At 5-foot-11, 185 pounds, he didn't look that strong. Yet he once lifted up the great Gordie Howe, removed him from the area in front of the goal and threw him to the ice. Howe was supposedly the strongest man in hockey.

To become a superstar before you're 21 means you have to start young. Bobby started as early as possible—he was on skates by the time he could walk. He had been born on March 20, 1948, in the little town of Parry Sound, Ontario, Canada, about 140 miles north of Toronto. It isn't

Bobby Orr takes the puck against the New York Rangers (far left) and drives past the Rangers' Jean Ratelle (left center). But he apparently loses the puck (right center) and comes to a stop (far right) as another Ranger looms on his left.

unusual in many parts of Canada for young-sters to be on skates before they're in nur-sery school. By the time Bobby was three, his father, Doug, noticed a kind of stubborn-ness about skating. "He'd take a stride," Doug recalled, "fall on his face, then get up and keep on skating."

Bobby attracted professional hockey scouts for the first time when he was 12, al-though it happened by accident. As a pre-liminary to an Eastern Professional Hockey League game, Bobby's bantam Parry Sound team was playing the Gananoque bantams. Two officials of the Boston Bruins, Wren Blair and Lynn Patrick, were there to watch two promising Gananoque youngsters. But Blair kept seeing out of the corner of his eye the moves of a little guy from Parry Sound. It was Orr.

Two years later Blair signed Bobby, bind-ing him to the Boston organization. Then Bobby was sent to the Oshawa junior team.

In hockey, this is not considered being a pro-fessional, even though the players and teams are subsidized by NHL organizations.

On Orr's first day at the Oshawa training camp, there was a roll call. Each player called out his name and position. When Bobby hollered out in a high-pitched voice that he was a defenseman, everybody laughed. Bobby was younger than everyone else, and weighed only 125 pounds. No one could imagine that he was strong enough to bodycheck someone who weighed 175 pounds or more. He soon proved differ-ently.

From the beginning at Oshawa he had major-league moves on the ice, and he was the team's biggest offensive threat. In three years he scored 101 goals, while still doing the job on defense. When the Bruins brought him up in 1966, they tried him for a few games at center, hoping to take greater advantage of his scoring talents. But

Bobby didn't care for it, and the Bruins agreed it was a bad idea.

"There's no sense in taking the game's best defenseman and playing him in another position," said Boston coach Harry Sinden. "It makes as much sense as playing Elizabeth Taylor in a boy's role."

The Bruins had finished last five of the last six seasons when Bobby joined them, but the fans sensed that Orr would be the one to lead them out of the cellar. In his first game in Boston, against Montreal, he scored on a long shot from the blue line, his first pro goal. The crowd jumped to its feet and gave him a standing ovation for several minutes. "Never heard anything like it," said Montreal coach Toe Blake.

Even the Bruins themselves considered the 18-year-old Orr their leader. They were constantly looking for him and yelling to him to take the puck. Still, Bobby couldn't do it alone and the Bruins finished last

again. Bobby was about all the Bruin fans had to cheer for. During one losing game late in the season a fan yelled to general manager Hap Emms: "Hey, Emms, why don't you trade Orr? He's making the rest of the Bruins look bad."

Bobby didn't enjoy hearing things like that, but people just couldn't help raving about him. He scored 41 points and was easily the league's Rookie of the Year. If there was an award for Rookie of the Century, he might have gotten that too. "Gordie Howe scores seven goals in his first year, but Orr scores 13 and he's a defenseman," said Chicago coach Billy Reay. "Is he the best rookie I've ever seen? I don't know. I think so."

Orr's impact on the Bruins began to pay off the next season. They got into the play-offs for the first time in nine years, even though Bobby had missed 28 games because of a leg injury. The Bruins rewarded Bobby at the end of the season with a three-year $400,000 contract. This time none of the Bruins begrudged Bobby his money; after all, they knew he would help them make more too. But they couldn't resist needling him. Once, a man delivered a large package to Bobby in the dressing room. "What's that?" said a teammate. "Your money for the week?" Bobby grinned, embarrassed.

The next year Orr began showing that no matter how much the Bruins paid him it would never be enough. He led Boston to a second-place finish during the regular season, won the James Norris Memorial Trophy as the league's top defenseman, and scored 64 points. Twenty-one of those points came on goals, a record for a defenseman. And three of those goals came in one night, giving Bobby the "hat trick," one of hockey's greatest achievements. When Bobby's third goal shot past Chicago goalie Ken Dryden, more than 50 fedoras, rainhats and fishing caps sailed down from the stands onto the Boston Garden ice.

People had long stopped being surprised by what Orr was capable of, but in 1969–70 he was simply overwhelming. The first two months of the season he had scored so many points that he seemed likely not only to win the scoring championship, but to set a record doing it. "When I came to Boston three seasons ago I thought Orr was an amazing skater," said teammate Phil Esposito, the defending scoring champion. "Last year I thought he was amazing and fantastic. This season he is amazing, fantastic . . . and I can't believe it."

Orr wound up with 120 points, six short of Esposito's NHL record, but almost twice as many points as any defenseman had ever scored before. And Bobby did get one big NHL record: 87 assists in one season.

Again the Bruins made the playoffs, but this time they weren't ready to settle for anything less than the Stanley Cup Championship itself. "Two years ago we got into the playoffs," said Orr, "and while we were congratulating ourselves the Canadiens beat us in four straight. Last year the Canadiens beat us in six games. I think all that is behind us. We've been here before—and lost. Now we're ready to win."

The Bruins' opponents in the first round were the New York Rangers. In the first game, with the Bruins momentarily short-handed because of a penalty, Orr dashed the length of the ice to score and Boston went on to win. In the second game Bobby set up the goal that put the game out of reach. New York won the next two on their own ice, but Bobby came back in games five and six with three goals and an assist to give Boston the victory in the best-of-seven series. In all, Bobby scored seven goals in the series, another record for a defenseman. "That Orr, he is impossible," said Rangers' star Rod Gilbert afterward. "Hockey is a team game, right? One man is not supposed to beat a whole team, right? But what else can I say? You saw it. One man beat the Rangers in this series."

It was more of the same in the next round. The Bruins were expected to have a rough time with Chicago, who had finished ahead of them during the regular season. But Orr, spectacular as always, helped dispose of them in four straight—even playing "goalie" by making several saves. The Bruins had only to beat St. Louis to win the Stanley Cup. Again they swept to victory in four straight games. Fittingly, Bobby scored the winning goal of the fourth game in a sudden-death overtime period.

The Bruins had won their last Stanley Cup in 1941, seven years before Bobby was even born. It had been a long wait, but with Bobby Orr on the team, the wait seemed almost worth it.

ARNOLD PALMER

In 1958 Arnold Palmer won the Masters, golf's most prestigious tournament, for the first time. He won it again in 1960, edging out Ken Venturi by a single stroke in an exciting finish. In 1961 he lost to Gary Player by one stroke in another dramatic ending. In 1962 he came to the Augusta National Club determined to win his third Masters title, as many as any man ever had won.

At the end of 72 holes, Palmer was tied with Player and Dow Finsterwald, forcing an 18-hole playoff on the following day. On the front nine, Finsterwald fell out of contention and Palmer faltered. With only nine holes to go, Palmer was five strokes over par and three strokes behind the chunky South African, Player. On the back nine, the 5-foot-11, 180-pound Pennsylvanian, brown hair tossing in the breeze, pursued his prize aggressively. Thousands in the gallery urged him on with tense, respectful silences as he lined up his shots and with cheers as the ball sailed down the fairway or rolled toward the cup.

At the 10th hole, Player missed the green and went one over par for a bogey. Meanwhile, Palmer sank a long, curling 25-foot putt for a birdie, pulling within a single stroke of Player. On 12, Player, still one stroke ahead, needed three putts and chalked up another bogey. Palmer dropped a four-footer for another birdie to take a one-stroke lead.

The sun-tanned, bull-shouldered Palmer strode aggressively from shot to shot, smiling sometimes when the fans made amusing comments. "Hey, what did ya do on the last hole?" a young fan called out. Stepping back from his next shot and studying the fan with mock severity, Arnie said, "Where were

Arnold Palmer watches the flight of his drive.

you?" As the fans laughed, Arnie smiled and lined up his three-foot putt on 13. He drilled it in for another birdie. Moving to the next tee, he rubbed his hands together and told his group, "Well, let's do us some good." He drove long, chipped up onto the green and snaked in a 16-foot putt for his third straight birdie.

Nothing seemed to disturb him. He was young and confident and at the top of his game. His playoff rivals, even the brilliant Player, seemed to regard him with awe. On 15, his drive was headed into the gallery, but it hit a spectator's chair and bounced back into the fairway. "Well," grinned Arnie, "it would appear this is my day." "Every day," sighed Finsterwald, "is your day." Palmer hit the green on his second shot and two-putted for his par.

On 16, Player missed a six-foot birdie putt and settled for par. Palmer smoothly stroked a 10-footer home for a birdie, and the South African admitted, "It's all over." The crowd cheered Palmer through the final two holes. With his five birdies in a stretch of seven holes going home, Arnie had won by three strokes, and as Player politely doffed his cap to Palmer, the fans applauded wildly. Arnie grinned and hurled his ball into the gallery, where the people fought for it as though it were a precious gem.

With that victory, Arnold Palmer established himself as the successor to Sam Snead and Ben Hogan as the new king of golf. When he won an unprecedented fourth Masters in 1964, by six strokes over Jack Nicklaus, Palmer placed himself among the immortals. He had won the U. S. Amateur title in 1954 and the U. S. Open title in 1960. He tied for the Open titles in 1962, 1963 and 1966, but lost playoffs. Through the 1960s, he failed to win only the Professional Golfers' Association (PGA) crown, the third of the major pro tournaments, but in both 1961 and 1962 he won the classic British Open.

In all, Palmer won approximately 50 major tourneys during the 1960s. But it was the way he won them which set him apart from the others. Striding aggressively from shot to shot, nervously hitching up his pants as he went, Arnie literally attacked courses. He gambled on difficult shots rather than playing safe. He won and he lost dramatically. He made "charge" a part of the golfing language as he came from behind with dramatic surges to win under pressure. He made golf seem a true athletic endeavor rather than a game for the rich and the old.

He became the first golfer ever to win more than a million dollars in purses, yet he remained under all circumstances a good-natured and appealing personality. He was always honest, even about his own failings. When he had struggled like a duffer on the ninth hole of the Los Angeles Open at Rancho Golf Course in 1961, promoter Al Franken proposed a plaque commemorating his incredible score of 12. Arnie unabashedly approved it. "What's more," he grinned, "I'll dedicate it."

The fans loved him, following him in such numbers they came to be called Arnie's Army. They even carried signs and banners dedicated to him around the course. At one Masters, three rooters paid a pilot to fly over the course in a plane trailing a "GO ARNIE GO" banner after him. During the afternoon, the pilot, also a fan, improvised his own messages of encouragement for different situations. "GO FOR IT," his banner read at one point when Palmer had a risky shot to make. Arnie grinned and said, "Guess I've got to go for it." And with the fans cheering him on, he did, and made it.

Even when his play tailed off in the last years of the '60s, Palmer remained the most popular pro on tour and drew the greatest galleries. It was partly because of his popularity that golf prospered until $100,000 tournaments became commonplace and nationally-televised play became a weekend habit with millions of viewers. For the first time golf was reaching the masses and gain-

Palmer urges a putt toward the cup—with help from his army of fans and admirers.

ing new popularity with the young.

The son of a Latrobe, Pennsylvania, golf pro, "Deac" Palmer, Arnie was born September 10, 1929. He started swinging a golf club at the age of four and by the time he was seven and eight years old he was spending every spare moment on a golf course. As the pro's son, he was in a position to challenge the older boys who were caddies, and he beat them regularly.

By the time he began to caddy, he could beat most of the club members. He gave up

baseball and football. "Somehow I felt golf had more thrills," he said. "And it had and always had one great charm: I was on my own. I did not have to depend on anybody else. Whether I won or lost, it was mine."

Palmer admits, "Without constant pressure from my teachers, I would never had done my school homework, but nobody had to urge me to do golfing homework. When something went wrong with my shots I couldn't wait to get back to the practice tee and go to work." He became a perfectionist.

He also became caddie master for his father at Latrobe. His dad later said that Arnie was the worst caddie master he ever had because the boy always was locking up the shop and going to the practice tee.

Arnie entered Wake Forest College with a friend, but when the friend was killed in an automobile accident, Palmer left school after his junior year and went into the Coast Guard. At 24, he got a job as a salesman and began to conquer the amateur golf circuit. He turned pro and eloped with his sweetheart, Winnie, because her parents did not think highly of the prospects of a traveling professional golfer. After the marriage, however, they loaned him $600 to help him get started.

In 1958, he won $42,000 on tour. Two years later, he led all money-winners in the game. In 1963, he won $128,230. Twenty years earlier Ben Hogan had been golf's leading money winner, earning only $13,-000. As late as 1953, only $34,000 went to the top winner. But golf had become a rich game. Through the 1960s, Palmer seldom won less than $100,000 a year and this was little compared to his earnings off the courses. His business manager Mark Mc-Cormack helped Palmer use his popularity to start golf equipment, clothing, and laundry businesses. Palmer finally sold his business empire for $6,000,000

Even after selling his business interests, Palmer remained active in them. He traveled so often and so far that he bought his own jet plane and learned to pilot it.

Palmer insists, however, "Money never was my incentive in golf. I play golf as well as I can because I like to win, and the money has come by accident." Although he claims he can shut business from his mind when it is time to play golf, he sometimes seemed distracted on the course and his play declined in the late 1960s. "I sometimes long for the old days," he once admitted, "when all I had to do was practice and play golf, practice and play golf."

As the 1970s began no single performer dominated the circuit as Palmer had in the first half of the 1960s. Palmer was past 40, old as athletes go, and he was troubled with a hip problem. Although Palmer had probably passed his peak, the memory of his clutch victories and the cheers of his huge army of admirers remains golden.

Palmer stands alone and dejected after missing a crucial putt in the 1965 Masters tournament.

FRANK ROBINSON

It was a cool sunny afternoon in early April and fewer than 13,000 persons had turned out to see the Baltimore Orioles open the 1966 baseball season. Frank Robinson shook his head as the Orioles came to bat in the first inning. This was his first game with Baltimore since being traded from Cincinnati over the winter. Looking at all the empty seats, Robinson wondered if this was a bad omen.

In ten years as a superstar with Cincinnati, Frank's heroics had attracted hundreds of thousands to come out and see him play. Now, only a handful of fans were on hand for his American League debut. "Maybe this is the beginning of the end for me," he thought as he walked to the plate after the first two Orioles had gone out.

Earl Wilson, a tough, aggressive competitor much like Robinson, was on the mound for Boston. Robinson leaned over the plate in his familiar crowding style, his head bent directly into the path of the strike zone. That dangerous batting stance had cost Robinson nearly 200 bruises from balls thrown by opposing pitchers. But try as he may, he couldn't hit as well standing any other way.

Wilson's first pitch smashed into Frank's right forearm. "Oh, no, here we go again," Robinson thought as he trotted to first base shaking off the pain. "At least, that's something that hasn't changed."

Moments later Robinson scored as his teammate Brooks Robinson, a star himself, slugged a Wilson pitch over the left field wall. When Frank went to bat in the third inning, he singled off Wilson. The next time up, Robinson smashed a Wilson fast ball over the right field screen and the Orioles

Frank Robinson hits another long drive. After a long career with the Cincinnati Reds, Robinson became a superstar for Baltimore.

went on to beat Boston 5–4 in 13 innings. "I've been hit plenty but never on opening day," Frank recalled after the game. "The homer evened up things."

Despite his good start, Robinson still wondered about his future. When Cincinnati owner Bill DeWitt had traded him the previous December, he claimed Robinson was getting old. It was true that Frank had been playing a long time. But at 30 he didn't think he was slowing down. After all, he had accumulated an enviable record in 10 years at Cincinnati. He had played in five All-Star games and averaged .303 at bat, 32 home runs a year and 101 runs-batted-in a year.

In the second game of the season, Frank hit another home run. The next day he hit another. By the end of the week he had his fourth and the Baltimore fans were excited. They hurried to Baltimore's Memorial Stadium by the thousands to watch the man destined to bring them a pennant.

On May 8, a record crowd of 49,516 turned out for a Sunday doubleheader. The Orioles were battling for first place against Cleveland. The crowd that day witnessed one of Robinson's—and Baltimore's—most dramatic moments ever. It came when Robinson batted for the first time in the second game.

Frank had already hit one home run in the first game to help give Baltimore an 8–2 victory. Now, with two out in the first inning of the second game, he faced the Indians' pitching ace, Luis Tiant. Tiant had not given up a run in his last 27 innings but the Orioles knew they had to beat him to take over first place.

Tiant threw a fast ball low and inside. Frank swung with all the force his 6-foot-1, 195-pound frame could muster and he literally hit the ball out of sight. As the spectators in the left field bleachers watched, the ball sailed over their heads. It landed in a parking lot 450 feet away from home plate and rolled another 100 feet before stopping. It was the first time anyone ever had hit a

After sweeping the 1966 World Series from the Dodgers in four games, the Orioles celebrate in the clubhouse. Frank Robinson hugs fellow star Brooks Robinson (back to camera).

home run out of Memorial Stadium and the crowd gave Frank a long standing ovation.

"It was a heck of a thing for the fans to do that," Robinson said later. "It hit me in a soft spot. It was the biggest ovation I ever saw any town give anybody."

But the ovations were just beginning in Baltimore for Frank Robinson. His exploits continued throughout the 1966 season as he led the Orioles to the American League pennant and a four game sweep of Los Angeles in the World Series. He led the league in average (.313), home runs (49) and runs-batted-in (118) and thus became only the 12th man in baseball history to win the Triple Crown. Frank capped the honors by being named Most Valuable Player in the American League. He had won the National League's MVP in 1961 and thus became the first man ever to win the MVP award in both leagues.

Since professional baseball began, few men have accomplished what Frank Robinson did in the 1960s. He was a superstar in two leagues, a man whose very presence inspired teammates toward great feats.

Frank was born in Beaumont, Texas, on August 31, 1935, but his family moved to Oakland, California, when he was small. As a youngster, he thought about little except baseball.

"I can't remember a hot meal from the time I was 12 years old until I signed with the Reds," he once recalled. "I'd get home from playing ball when everybody else was in bed and there would be my supper in a cold pot on the stove." His family didn't like him to play baseball all the time and constantly were after him to get a good job.

Robinson was first spotted by Cincinnati scout Bobby Mattick when still a skinny 14-year-old playing American Legion Junior baseball. Among his Legion teammates was a youngster named Vada Pinson. Pinson

Robinson waits in the on-deck circle for his turn at bat.

later followed Frank to the Reds and became his closest friend.

The Reds waited until Robinson had graduated from McClymonds High School in June of 1953 before signing him to a contract. His bonus was $3,000, a far cry from the $100,000 he would earn by the end of the decade.

Although only 17 years old, Frank was an immediate sensation with Cincinnati's farm club at Ogden, Utah, in the Pioneer League. In 1954, he moved to Columbia, S.C., in the Sally League where he hit 25 homers and batted in 110 runs. But returning to Columbia the following year, Frank was a disappointment.

First, he was slowed by an arm ailment he had contracted while playing winter ball in Puerto Rico. Secondly, he found it difficult to handle the racial situation of a black man in the south. It was the lowest point of his life but the Reds were not disappointed. They decided to promote him to the major leagues in 1956 and they never were sorry.

As a rookie, he set the combative, challenging style which was to mark the rest of his career. He made the National League All-Star team at mid-season, gaining praise for his defensive outfield work as well as his hitting. By the end of the year he had set a new league home run record for rookies with 38. For his standout performance he was named Rookie of the Year.

In 1957 he hit over .300 for the first time. However, before the 1958 season started, an incident almost ended Robinson's career —and his life. During a spring exhibition game, Frank was hit on the left temple, just below the protective batting helmet, by a pitch thrown by Washington's Camilo Pascual. He was carried off the field and spent several days in the hospital.

Frank recovered physically but not emotionally. By July he was hitting under .250 and had just 8 homers and 23 RBIs. Then, suddenly, he reversed course. In the last 80 games he hit 23 homers and 60 RBIs. In recalling that 1958 beaning, Robinson is well aware that his emotional reaction salvaged his career.

"At the beginning, I kept telling myself I wasn't afraid," he said. "Still, I couldn't keep from rolling back on my heels every time a pitcher curved me. Then all of a sudden I wasn't falling back anymore. I guess I got so mad at myself I didn't give a damn what happened."

In 1961, Robinson sparked Cincinnati to the pennant by batting .323, hitting 37 homers and driving in 124 runs. He was even better in 1962 when he almost single-handedly took the Reds to another pennant, setting career highs with a .342 average and 136 RBIs. He also smashed 39 homers.

However, even as he continued to rally Cincinnati in the 1960s, Frank was having difficulty achieving the recognition that went to such National League stars as Willie Mays. Undoubtedly, his aggressive style caused some resentment but Frank always took the snubs in stride.

"Baseball isn't a popularity contest," he said. "Some players are afraid of losing friends. Not me. I'm not out there to win friends, just ball games, and I'll do that any way I can."

However, with the trade to Baltimore and his subsequent accomplishments, Robinson finally gained the recognition he deserved. As the decade ended, Frank was still among the best power hitters in the game. In 1969 he hit .308 with 32 home runs and 100 RBIs and carried the Orioles to another pennant. Those 32 homers gave him a 14-year total of 450 and placed him 12th on baseball's all-time home run list.

"I've had many good years in baseball," Frank has recalled, "but from a personal standpoint, 1966 gave me my greatest satisfaction. Not only had Cincinnati traded me but a lot of people had been skeptical of my ability. I proved myself that year."

PETE ROSE

Pete Rose of the Cincinnati Reds was on second base, with teammate Vada Pinson at the plate. At the crack of the bat Rose streaked toward third. As he reached the base he saw the first baseman drop the throw from the infield. Rose didn't hesitate. He rounded third, put his head down and raced for home.

Guarding the plate was Braves catcher Gene Oliver, who was three inches taller and 25 pounds heavier than Rose. Pete knew he couldn't bowl him over, so he had two other choices: he could try to hook slide and touch a piece of the plate with his toe or he could dive head first and try to reach between Oliver's legs to touch the plate. Rose decided to dive, and somehow he managed to score. But he also banged his face against the catcher's shin guard. When Pete got up his face was sliced raw.

Why did he go in head first?

"I thought I could get there quicker," he said simply.

Getting there quicker is Pete Rose's trademark. In the '60s he was the only ballplayer who ever *ran* to first base after a base on balls. "The faster I get to first," he explained, "the faster I can get to second." The first time the New York Yankees saw him do it, in a 1963 exhibition game, they couldn't believe it. "My gosh!" said Yankee pitcher Whitey Ford. "It's Charley Hustle!" The nickname stuck.

Most ballplayers didn't care for Rose's tactics at first. They thought he was trying to show them up, and they called him a "hot dog" or show-off, about the worst thing one ballplayer could say about another. But Rose's hustle paid off. He was voted the National League's Rookie of the Year in 1963,

Pete Rose heads for first base after hitting the ball, showing the hustle that is his trademark.

at the age of 22. "He went from most valuable hot dog to most valuable player," said one observer.

People have been cheering Rose ever since. Between 1965 and 1969 he got over 200 hits four different years, and in '68 and '69 he won league batting titles. He entered the 1970s with a career average well over .300. Ted Williams, baseball's last .400 hitter, thought Rose might hit .400 someday.

Rose wasn't sure he could live up to Williams' prediction. But Rose's roommate, Tommy Helms knew Pete would be thinking about it every minute. Many a morning Helms has awakened to find Pete standing in front of a mirror, swinging an imaginary bat. "I've never seen anybody with so much enthusiasm and so much energy," Helms has said. "Just being with him makes you tired."

For Pete Rose, "Baseball is like a disease. It's what's inside me." Like many diseases, this one was contagious. Pete picked it up from his father, Harry, a semi-pro baseball and football player. Pete was born on April 14, 1941, in Cincinnati, and when he was three years old his father went downtown to buy shoes for Pete and his sister. His father returned—not with shoes, but with a catcher's mitt for Pete. "Some kids are raised on rice and potatoes," Pete would say years later. "I was raised on athletics."

With his father watching over him, Pete was a Little League catcher at eight and he learned to switch-hit at ten. Pete and his father also went to Reds games, where Pete could learn how the pros did it. Once Pete saw Enos Slaughter hustle for an extra base. "That's the kind of ballplayer I want to be," Pete said to his father. "Always running."

When Pete was a sophomore at Western Hills High School, his coach shifted him from catcher to second base because he thought Pete was too small to be a catcher. But lack of size didn't keep Pete from getting a pro contract two years later. The Reds scout who signed him happened to be his uncle, Buddy Bloebaum. Bloebaum knew that Pete's father had been slow to reach his adult playing weight and he expected that Pete would continue to grow too.

Pete graduated from high school on a Friday in 1960, signed a baseball contract on Saturday and left for Geneva of the Class D New York-Pennsylvania League on Monday. The last thing his father said to him was, "Keep hustling," and during the months to follow he would end each letter with the same advice.

Pete followed his father's advice. He also grew as Buddy Bloebaum expected. Within three years he stood 5-foot-11 and weighed 190 pounds. And he was a major leaguer, again getting there quicker than most people expected. One night during spring training in 1963, a Cincinnati sportswriter was sitting around with ten Reds players. He handed out ten slips of paper, ten pencils, and asked each player to list the 25 men they expected to make the regular-season squad. Only one player wrote down Rose's name. The player who did was Don Blasingame. Blasingame was right. Rose made the squad and won a starting job—Blasingame's job at second.

Opposing players getting their first look at Rose that season figured he was mainly a singles and doubles hitter. But Pete also made them respect his power. Early in one game San Francisco center fielder Willie Mays caught a fly by Rose. As they crossed paths at the end of the inning, Rose said, "You better play me deeper."

"Man," said Willie, "what are you talking about? You can't hit that ball over my head."

The next time Rose came up he smashed the ball well over Mays's head, for one of his nine triples that year. Willie never played Rose shallow again.

Pete's batting average went over .300 for the first time in 1965 when he batted .312.

During his first three years Pete played second base. After that, he played a new position every year. In 1966 he was moved to third base to make room for Tommy Helms at second. The next season he played left field and in 1968 he played right. Many players would have been upset by all the shifting, but Rose took it all in stride. The Reds knew he would continue to be an All-Star no matter where he played.

By 1968, Rose was competing for the National League batting title. In the last weekend of play he was neck-and-neck with Matty Alou of the Pirates. Both were hitting over .330. Then Pete fell into a slump, getting only one hit in seven at-bats in a 15-inning game. The next day Pete took 25 minutes of extra batting practice. Helms stood on the sidelines and needled him, hoping it would anger Pete into action with the bat. "You swing like a girl," he shouted.

Something worked. That day in the next-to-last game of the season, Rose went 5-for-5. But on the same day Alou went 4-for-4. Now the batting title depended on the last game. Rose and the Reds were playing the Giants. In the very first inning Rose smashed a double. It was his only hit of the day, but it was all he needed. Alou went 0-for-4 and Rose won his first batting crown, hitting .335 to Alou's .332.

Defending the title in 1969 was no easier than winning it the first time. The Reds had one of the finest hitting teams in baseball history, and through the first half of the season four or five of Pete's teammates had better averages than he. But he finished like a true champion the last two months and again won the title on the last day. The man he had to beat out this time was Roberto Clemente of the Pirates, who already had won four batting titles. Pete clinched the title with a bunt single in the eighth inning of the last game of the season. His final average was .348 to Clemente's .345.

For Pete Rose, his second batting championship was the last step toward a cherished goal. Since he was a rookie, he had been telling people that he would be the first singles-hitter to receive a $100,000 salary. He received a $100,000 contract for the 1970 season.

When asked why being first was so important to him, Pete would say, "I gotta, that's all, I just gotta." It didn't seem to be much of an answer, but anyone who had ever seen Pete Rose run to first on a base-on-balls knew it was answer enough.

Rose waits for a pitch during batting practice, keeping in shape to earn his place as the highest paid singles-hitter in baseball.

BILL RUSSELL

Early in 1956, coach Red Auerbach of the Boston Celtics called an old friend who lived in San Francisco. The friend was Fred Scolari, who once had played for Red. Auerbach wanted Scolari's opinion about a 6-foot-9 center at San Francisco University named Bill Russell.

"This kid can't shoot to save himself," Scolari said, "but he can get the ball for you. He's the best I ever saw."

Red thought Scolari must be exaggerating —Scolari had seen and played against George Mikan, who was then pro basketball's greatest center.

"If you want me to put it in writing," Scolari insisted, "I'll put it in writing. If you can get Russell, grab him. They'll be talking about him long after you and I are gone."

By the end of the season Russell had led San Francisco to its second straight national collegiate title. The team had set a record of 55 straight victories and Russell was a unanimous All-America choice. Auerbach was convinced. Without ever having seen Russell play in person, Auerbach traded two of his stars—Ed Macauley and Cliff Hagan —to St. Louis for the draft rights to Russell.

The rest is history. Boston won the pro championship in Russell's first year, and won it ten more times in Russell's 13-year career. No athlete in any sport was as consistent a winner as Russell. At the end of the 1960s he was voted the greatest athlete of the decade, beating out Willie Mays, Johnny Unitas, Bobby Hull and Arnold Palmer.

No one was more eager to give Russell credit for the Celtics' success than his own teammates. "Despite the rest of us," said Bob Cousy, who was the Celtics' playmaker during much of Russell's career and one of the greatest guards in history, "the Celtics never won anything until they got Russell. As a pro, I never saw anyone meet a challenge as well as Russ did. And a lot of it was pride.

"He simply couldn't allow himself to lose and still live with himself. He never repeated a mistake. If you took Russell off the Celtics and put him on almost any other team, he would have made that team a contender. I can't think of anyone else you could say that about."

Russell also revolutionized the game by perfecting a new kind of defense. Though he was seldom, if ever, the biggest man on the court, he blocked shots with the greatest sense of timing ever seen. A player would drive for the basket, thinking the coast was clear. Suddenly, as he started to lay up the ball, a long, thin arm would come out of nowhere to knock the ball away. Once this happened to a player a few times, Russell had the advantage. At that point Bill didn't even have to move a muscle; just the *threat* of his being there was enough to affect his opponent.

An example of Russell's contribution to the Celtics came in a game late in 1965. It was just another regular season game, one of nearly a thousand Russell was to play. Russell had been on the bench for most of the first three quarters, resting an injured leg. He and Auerbach had agreed Bill only would go on if the Celtics needed him. With two minutes left in the third period, the time came. The Celtics trailed the Lakers, 85–81. Russell went in for seven minutes. He rebounded fiercely and knocked away a pass that forced the Lakers to lose the ball on a 24-second violation. When Bill went back to the bench, Boston led, 96–92.

Bill Russell goes up to block a shot by Walt Bellamy, showing the defensive skill that revolution-ized the game.

Suddenly the game reversed itself again. Three straight times the Celtics missed their first shot and lost the rebound. With 3:05 remaining and the score tied at 102, Russell went back in. Bringing the ball downcourt he fed a perfect pass to Sam Jones as Jones broke for the basket. Jones scored and the Celtics went ahead. Russell got the next defensive rebound, started a fast break and John Havlicek hit from 20 feet. In a minute and 20 seconds, Boston had made three straight baskets. The Lakers scrambled and scored twice, but the possible tie-making shot by Rudy LaRusso was blocked by Russell. The Celtics got the ball and, finally, the game—108–106.

In ten minutes of play Russell had grabbed ten rebounds and provided a perfect demonstration of how to be the most valuable player on the court without scoring a point.

Russell wasn't a great scorer, but he was a consistent one. His best average was 18.9 in 1961–62. His career average was slightly

more than 15. He even joked about his occasional lack of accuracy. "They still call this club 'Four shooters and Russell,' " he once said. Yet when the Celtics needed a big basket late in the game, his shooting was no joke to the other team. His lefthanded hook was usually deadly in the clutch.

Russell was at his best when he was presented with a challenge. He proved it in his classic rivalry with Wilt Chamberlain. The first time they faced each other was on November 7, 1959. Russell was starting his fourth NBA season, and his reputation was on the line against the giant rookie. He outrebounded Wilt, 35–28, and Chamberlain scored only 12 times in 38 shots, far below his usual accuracy from the field. Most important, the Celtics won.

There were times, of course, when no one could stop Wilt, including Russell. But overall, the rivalry was one-sided where it counted most—in the final score. They met many times in the playoffs, with Wilt playing at various times for Philadelphia, San Francisco and Los Angeles. But only once—in the 1967 Eastern Division finals—did Russell and the Celtics lose. In fact, during Russell's career the Celtics won 28 playoff series and lost only two.

Many of Russell's contributions to the Celtics were "intangible." General manager Eddie Donovan of the New York Knicks explained that when he said: "The best part of Bill Russell never shows in the box score. You have to know a little about the way the game should be played, and then watch Russell night after night, to really appreciate him."

One intangible Russell brought to the Celtics was his leadership. On the court or

Russell stretches his 6-foot-9 frame as he comes down with a rebound.

in the locker room, the Celtics looked to Russell for inspiration. Thus, when Red Auerbach decided to retire as coach at the end of the 1966 season, it wasn't surprising that Bill Russell was named the new coach, becoming the first black man to coach a major-league team in any sport. He also continued to play.

Being a player-coach is the toughest job in sports, because it is two jobs. In the heat of the battle Russell sometimes forgot to make substitutions, leaving players in after they had become exhausted. But he learned gradually to adjust to playing and coaching at the same time.

When the Celtics were beaten in 1966–67 by a great Philadelphia team, many people thought the Boston dynasty was dead. "Maybe we are dead," Russell told his players at a dinner a couple of days after the final defeat. "But that's only till next season. Then the Celtics will be very much alive."

The following summer, Russell set about bringing the Celtics back to good health. One day he assembled several of his veterans and told them: "There's a century of basketball experience in this room. I expect you fellows to help me."

After Russell's speech the players felt freer to criticize and to offer advice. By the end of the season the Celtics were champions again, beating the Lakers for the title in six games. And Bill Russell had proven that he was not only a winning player, he was a winning coach.

No more proof was needed, but Russell felt compelled to prove it one more time in 1968–69. That task almost turned out to be too much. Russell was 35 now, and the rest of the team was weakening. The Celtics finished only fourth in the Eastern Division, just barely making the playoffs. But the playoffs had always been Russell's special time of the year, and he and his team

Coach Bill Russell watches from the bench during 1968.

seemed to summon one last bit of strength. They beat Philadelphia in the first round, then disposed of the young New York Knicks in the second round.

In the finals the Celtics met the Los Angeles Lakers—Wilt Chamberlain, Jerry West, Elgin Baylor and the rest. Los Angeles won the first two games, but Russell and his aging team won four of the last five and became the first team ever to come back from an 0–2 deficit to win a championship series. Russell had done it again.

During the summer of 1969 he announced his retirement. Bill Russell had gone out the same way he had come in—as a winner, the greatest winner sports had ever known.

JIM RYUN

Jim Ryun works out with the track team at East High School in Wichita. He broke four minutes in the mile before he graduated.

Jim Ryun, 16 years old, was discouraged. For months he had been running in the early morning hours, logging 100 to 120 miles a week. He had run in the snow and ice of winter and in the sticky heat of summer. He had been running by himself through the deserted streets and fields of Wichita, Kansas, and a feeling of loneliness had crept over him. Now, as he got out of his track suit, he wondered out loud whether the whole thing was worth it.

His coach at Wichita East High School, Bob Timmons, was there in the locker room. He heard Jim's question, and he understood. He knew how difficult such a training routine could be on a young boy. But he also knew that if Jim wanted to reach his goal of someday being the world's greatest mile runner, there could be no shortcuts. So he explained this to Jim and said he thought the training and even the loneliness was worth it. Jim agreed and gained new strength from the reassurance of his coach.

In many ways Jim Ryun had already come too far to turn back. Born on April 29, 1947, Jim had more than his share of physical problems while growing up. He was allergic to dust and feathers, he squinted from being nearsighted, and he had a hernia operation. He also got appendicitis.

"I was home one day when I became very ill," he has recalled. "I began to vomit. I tried to eat, but I couldn't keep anything down. We got the doctor. An hour later my appendix was removed. I was so sick I passed out when I checked into the hospital. They didn't have to use anesthesia. If I'd waited four or five hours longer, I wouldn't have lived. Then I got peritonitis. I was pretty sick."

Jim didn't get serious about competitive

sports until his sophomore year of high school. At an assembly, the school athletic program was explained. Jim decided to go out for the cross-country squad, even though he hadn't been fast enough to make his junior high school track team.

Jim was 6-foot-1, and weighed 145 pounds —he was all arms and legs. In his first practice mile he finished 14th and ran 5:38. But by the following spring Jim had lowered his time to 4:26.4 and Coach Timmons realized he had a real prospect. That's when the training program for Ryun was stepped up. Their goal was to make Jim the first high school boy to break four minutes. It was an incredible goal, considering that when Jim was born the *world* record was set at 4:01.4. The four-minute barrier hadn't been broken until 1954, and then it took a man in his middle 20s, Roger Bannister, to do it.

But in the summer of 1963, when Jim was just a couple of months past his 16th birthday, he showed how close he was to four minutes. He ran the mile in 4:08.2, and a fine 1:54.5 half-mile at the same meet.

At the end of Jim's junior year, Bob Timmons was hired as the track coach at Kansas University. Jim's new coach became J. D. Edmiston, whose approach was different from Timmons'. Jim liked Timmons very much, but he also liked the change. "Mr. Edmiston made me make a few decisions on my own," Jim said. "Everybody before had told me what to do. Not just about track, but about life in general."

In the spring of 1964 Jim was invited to join a select field of seven other runners in the mile race at the Compton Relays in California. In the group were world record-holder Peter Snell of New Zealand and America's top hope, Jim Beatty. Halfway through the race, Ryun was holding his own, running strongly in the middle of the pack. Suddenly, he was shoved off the track. The

startled young runner waited until everyone passed him before he resumed running. Not surprisingly, he wound up dead last. But his time was 3:59! At the age of 17 he had broken the four-minute mile.

That September, Jim went to the Olympic Trials in California, hoping to earn one of the three spots in the 1500-meter run on the American team for the Tokyo Olympics. (1500 meters is about 115 yards less than a mile.) It didn't seem likely he'd make it. Dyrol Burleson, Tom O'Hara and Jim Grelle all were much older and were experienced in world-class meets. Grelle, in fact, had won the 1500 in the U. S.-Russian meet earlier that summer and was so confident of making the Olympic team that he announced, "I've already bought my wife a roundtrip ticket to Tokyo."

With 150 yards to go in the qualifying race, Ryun was seventh and last. At that point he said to himself, "I've put in an awful lot of work to finish this way. Try harder."

Jim began his finishing sprint for which he was to become famous. He passed three men, with the tape fast approaching. Burleson and O'Hara were out of reach, but he came shoulder-to-shoulder with Grelle and just edged him out at the tape qualifying for the trip to Tokyo.

At the Tokyo Olympics Jim caught a bad cold and finished ninth in the ten-man field. The trip was an apparent failure. But Jim benefitted from the total experience. He knew that by 1968 he'd be 21 years old, and at his peak. The previous Olympic competition would help him next time.

He was also thrilled just to have made the trip to Japan. Competing in track gave him a rare chance to get a broader view of the world around him.

In the spring of 1965, Jim returned to the Compton Relays and ran against two men he knew all too well—Peter Snell and Jim Grelle. Jim finished in 3:56 but he was two steps behind the two great milers. It was his best time yet and it was obvious that he was the least tired of the three at the end of the race. Jim rushed to congratulate Snell on his victory, but the New Zealander ignored Jim. The snub may have been unintentional, however, because later Snell praised him highly.

Another rematch came three weeks later at the National AAU Meet in San Diego. This time Jim went in with a firm plan, based largely on what the last race had taught him. He would try to take the lead in the last quarter, then start sprinting if someone challenged him.

With 300 yards to go in the race Jim had to revise his plan. He found himself slightly boxed in, and Snell was still ahead of him. Jim opened up, his long, racehorse legs cutting down the distance in large chunks. With 150 yards to go, he passed Snell. But now Grelle was coming on strong. He pulled even with Jim but then fell back again. Incredibly, Snell now made another try for the lead and he and Ryun sprinted the last 50 yards. At the end, Jim was the winner by several steps. His time was 3:55.3, the fastest ever run by an American. Snell, a gallant loser, hugged Ryun. Fifteen minutes later, on national television, Ryun told the audience how he felt during the race. "All at once I was in front," he said, "and it scared me to death."

That fall Jim enrolled at the University of Kansas on a full track scholarship, excited at the idea of working with Coach Timmons again. The rugged early-morning grind continued and Jim's goal was now the world record. At times, he admitted, he still thought "about how nice it would be home in bed." But other times he felt only joy from running on the Kansas plains. "I look at the sky and the trees and flowers, or just the grass," he said, "and I feel clean and pure."

By the spring of 1966, Jim had been trained to a fine, sharp edge. He proved it with the greatest string of mile and half-mile races that the world had ever seen. He began with the Compton Relays, where he won the mile in 3:53.7, just a tenth of a second behind Frenchman Michel Jazy's world record.

Six days later he entered a meet in Terre Haute, Indiana, to run the half-mile. It was only the seventh competitive half-mile of his life, and in the preliminaries he felt terrible. Even in the first quarter-mile of the final Jim didn't seem up to form, running a slow 53.1. At that point he was worried even about placing.

"Then with 300 yards left I figured if I could go hard, I might win," he explained later. "I drove, and I turned around, and I was ten yards ahead of everybody else. I could not believe it. I kept moving, and then I was 20 yards ahead. The race surprised me. I realized I had a lack of confidence in myself."

Jim's time was 1:44.9, breaking Snell's world record of 1:45.1. Now people looked forward to Jim's next big mile race. He seemed completely ready to grab *that* world record too.

Five weeks later, at Berkeley, California, the moment came. And the amazing thing was, it came in a runaway race, when there were no competitors forcing him to run harder. Toward the end, Jim's closest rival, Cary Weisiger, was 80 yards behind. But Jim wanted the record desperately, so he summoned up all the speed and strength and endurance he had gained from those lonely hours of training. He crossed the finish line in 3:51.3, smashing Jazy's record by more than two seconds.

Ryun crosses the line in the fastest mile he ever ran, at the AAU championships at Bakersfield, California in June 1967. His time was 3:51.1.

Jim was thrilled and happy by the record, of course, but he confessed he wasn't "knocked out" by it. What he wanted even more, he said, was to win in the 1968 Olympics at Mexico City.

If the Olympics had been held right then, there's little doubt Ryun would have gotten his gold medal. But in the next two years Jim's old problems—illness and injury—came back to haunt him. First he got mononucleosis, forcing him to stop training for a long, long time. Before he regained all his strength he still did well enough at the Olympic Trials in Lake Tahoe to win a spot on the American team. But the night after the

trials he came down with a kidney infection. That too set his training back. When he returned he pulled a muscle in his right leg that cost him valuable days of training.

When Jim got to Mexico City, he couldn't break 70 seconds for a practice quarter-mile. He felt defeated, and threatened to give up before the race. He ran well enough in the first heat, and he qualified in the second heat as well, but he also reinjured the muscle.

Warming up for the finals, Jim still wasn't sure he could run. He also knew that even if he were in perfect shape he would be at a disadvantage in the rarefied air of Mexico City's 7,300-foot altitude. Ryun's chief ri-

Ryun works out in high altitude near Alamosa, Colorado, preparing for the 1968 Olympics in Mexico City. His success as a runner depended on long hours of solitary practice.

val, Kip Keino of Kenya, had done all his training in the mountains of his homeland, and his huge lungs were much more accustomed to the thin air. In a long race like the 1500, that could make all the difference.

Jim stayed off Keino's pace in the first lap and a half; he was afraid that if he tried to keep up with him, his leg would give out. With two laps to go, Jim made his move and closed the gap a bit. But Keino was tireless and won by 25 yards in the Olympic record time of 3:34.9.

Ryun won the silver medal for the U. S. in the excellent time of 3:37.8. He naturally was disappointed, yet in many ways his second-place finish was a greater tribute to

his talent and spirit than the dozens of races he had won in the past.

Jim continued to compete in 1969, but he could no longer kid himself. He simply didn't have the same motivation to put in the long hours of training. He hinted that he might try out for the '72 Olympic team, but he insisted that most of his energies would go toward a career in photography.

Jim Ryun had already revolutionized the mile. He had shown that a person didn't have to wait until his mid-20s to reach his peak as a distance runner. He proved that if a boy was man enough to endure the loneliness of the long-distance runner, he could *run* like a man, too.

GALE SAYERS

Gale Sayers of the Chicago Bears took the pitchout and began running to his left. When he saw he couldn't turn the outside corner, he decided to cut back inside. Just as he planted his right foot to make the cut, it happened. Kermit Alexander of the San Francisco 49ers hit Gale with a low, rolling block. With Sayers' cleats anchored in the turf, it was impossible for him to fall normally. Sayers' right knee took the full force of the blow, bending 90 degrees sideways.

Sayers went down in agony. He looked up at Alexander and cried, "The knee's gone." Alexander was horrified. He was a friend of Sayers', and the block he had thrown was perfectly clean. But with that one block he had possibly ended the career of pro football's greatest running back. Sayers was only 25, perhaps still a year or two from his prime. Vince Lombardi, the long-time coach of the Green Bay Packers, had called him "the most sensational runner of our time."

Now, in the 1968 season, he had seemed to be on his way to his greatest year. In the first eight games he had gained 856 yards rushing, and his average of 5.3 yards a carry was better than Jimmy Brown's NFL record. In the ninth game, against San Francisco, Gale had gained 32 yards in his first ten carries. But his 11th carry spelled disaster.

Only hours after he was helped off the field he was in surgery to repair the torn ligaments and the ruptured cartilage. Speed was vital. "You wait 24 hours after one of those things," said the surgeon, Dr. Theodore Fox, "and it would be like trying to stitch together two bags of cornmeal mush."

The operation took three hours. When Gale regained consciousness, the doctor told

Gale Sayers is carried off the field on a stretcher after injuring his knee in 1968. The injury threatened to end his career.

him the operation had succeeded. "You wouldn't lie to me?" Gale asked. Then he began repeating the question, each time in a louder voice, until he was screaming, *"You wouldn't lie to me?"* The doctor assured him that all was well, but he also said that the hard part was just beginning.

Gale understood. Long hours, weeks and months lay ahead in rehabilitating the knee. Gale began by discarding his crutches a week after the operation. A month later, when the cast was removed, he exercised three times a day and even borrowed the Bears' weight machine to use at home. By mid-January, Gale was jogging.

He didn't need extra incentive to work hard, but he got it anyway. A Chicago sportswriter wrote one day that running backs rarely return to top form after a knee injury, and suggested that Sayers might have to play another position. Gale was furious when he read the article. "I saved it," he said, months later, "because when I do come back as a runner, I'm going to show it to him. *I will be back.*"

In late February, Dr. Fox and Gale went out to a soccer field. Gale cut to his left. Then he cut to his right. Finally, he ran straight at the doctor, planted his weight firmly on his right foot, cut to the left and shot past. They both smiled. "If there were a game this Sunday," said Dr. Fox, "you'd play."

Gale could hardly wait for training camp to open in July, to erase any doubts about his knee holding up when he was tackled. On the first day, he insisted on playing in the scrimmage. He carried the ball six times with no ill effects. Later in camp, he got hit as hard on one play as he'd ever been hit. But he bounced right up. "And it was in the legs," said quarterback Virgil Carter. "If he can take that, we aren't worried."

Sayers pretended to most people that he wasn't worried, either, but he finally admitted otherwise a couple of hours before the first exhibition game. "I think about it," he said, referring to the knee. "I never stop thinking about it. I know it's fine, but I think about it."

Both the opponent and the weather were designed to give Gale a full test that night. The Bears were playing the Washington Redskins, who were playing their first game under coach Vince Lombardi. When the teams took the field, there was a driving rainstorm that had already dotted the field with puddles.

Almost as if it were fated, the opening kickoff came down to Sayers. He took it on his six-yard line and shot straight up the middle. One Redskin broke through the wedge of Bears. Sayers gave him his great head-and-shoulders fake and was past him without losing a step. At the Redskin 40 another defender angled in on Sayers. Gale fought him off with his left arm and finally stepped out of bounds on the Redskin 25. On his first play since the accident he had gone 69 yards, and showed he had lost none of his speed.

Gale played sparingly in the mud and rain the rest of the game. He didn't have to endure much hitting, and he knew that until he did—and was able to survive it—his comeback wouldn't be complete. But he was satisfied with this beginning. He was sure that by the end of the season he would prove that he was as good as ever.

Sayers couldn't stand the thought of being just another average halfback, and who could blame him? Nearly all his life he had been an exceptional athlete. He was born in Wichita, Kansas, and moved to Omaha, Nebraska, when he was ten. At Omaha Central High School he made the all-state football team two straight years. He received over 100 college offers before deciding to attend the University of Kansas. People in Omaha were upset that he didn't choose the

Sayers leads the Minnesota Vikings on a 96-yard chase as he heads for one of his 21 touchdowns during his rookie season.

University of Nebraska. Some people thought Kansas must have offered him more than a scholarship.

But Gale's reasons were perfectly valid. At the time of his enrollment, in 1961, Kansas was turning out better teams than Nebraska. Gale felt he would have a better chance of being noticed by the pros if he was on a winning team. He also was attracted to Kansas coach Jack Mitchell. "He seemed like somebody I could trust," said Gale, "and that's just what he was. He helped me a lot in adjusting to college that first year."

Ironically, the longest run of Sayers' college career came against Nebraska. Gale, a junior, ran 99 yards from scrimmage. The rest of his college statistics were just as impressive. He averaged 6.5 yards a carry and broke most of the conference rushing records. He was named to most All-America

teams both as a junior and as a senior.

The 6-foot, 200-pound Sayers was drafted by the Bears of the NFL and Kansas City Chiefs of the AFL. Kansas City owner Lamar Hunt offered a lot of money, but Gale turned it down and later said jokingly, "When millionaires start opening the door for me, I get suspicious."

On December 1, 1964, Gale signed a three-year, $150,000 contract with the Bears. "I want to play with the best and against the best," said Gale. And he dazzled the entire NFL right from the start of the '65 season. He did it not just with speed, but with something more. Jack Mitchell knew what it was, because he had watched it for three years at Kansas. "He keeps his speed under control because he has balance, too," said Mitchell. "That's what sets him apart from the pack."

In the next-to-last game of the season,

Returning after his injury, Gale pulls away from Detroit's Lem Barney during the 1969 season.

Gale had his greatest day ever in football. It had rained much of the week and Chicago's Wrigley Field was a mess. But neither the mud nor the 49ers could stop Sayers. On the Bears' first play he took a screen pass on his own 20 and went 80 yards for the score. It was his 16th touchdown of the year. Then, in the closing five minutes of the half, he scored twice on end runs. One was from the San Francisco 21, the other from the seven.

Gale got his fourth touchdown on a pitchout early in the third quarter. By now the game was no contest. All interest focused on Sayers, who was just one short of Lenny Moore's NFL record of 20 touchdowns for a season.

Sayers' record-tying touchdown was an easy one compared to the others of the day. But it did display another of his assets—his strength. He crashed into the middle of the 49er line and scored from one yard out.

Midway through the fourth quarter Gale got another chance to handle the ball. He took a punt on his own 15 and spurted straight ahead. As the 49ers began pursuit, he swerved to the left. Then, without losing speed, he cut right across the grain of the pursuit and shot into the end zone. It was his sixth touchdown for the day, a feat equaled only twice in NFL history. And it was his 21st TD of the year, a league record. For the first time that day the normally quiet Sayers showed some emotion. He flipped the ball into the air, clapped his hands and skipped toward his teammates before sprinting back to the bench.

Afterward the Bears gave Sayers the game ball for the second time that season. It was the first time a Bear had ever received two in one year. "But what could we do?" said owner-coach George Halas. "That was the greatest game of football I've ever seen a man play."

In the season's final game, Gale added another touchdown to his total. He was a runaway winner for Rookie of the Year. During the rest of the 1960s neither Gale nor anyone else came close to his 22 touchdowns. But Gale now was adding other records. In 1967 he broke the record for total offense in one season with 2,440 yards. By 1969 he was the only player to have scored as many as six touchdowns on kickoff returns.

Sayers continued to gain new lines in the record book after his knee injury. In 1969, in spite of the Bears' weak offensive line, he led the NFL in rushing with 1,032 yards. And as if to prove his durability, he carried the ball more times—236—than anyone else in the league.

Gale's return as the king of football's running backs brought to mind what George Seals had said during the summer. "Many athletes come back from knee injuries lacking quite a bit," said Seals, a Bears offensive lineman. "I feel if Sayers comes back, he'll be the one that comes back all the way."

George Seals knew his man pretty well.

DON SCHOLLANDER

Don Schollander became a member of the famous Santa Clara Swim Club of California in January 1962. Don was not quite 16, but already he seemed to be a potential threat to world freestyle records.

Soon after joining the club, Don was handed a little notebook by coach George Haines. "Take this," the coach said, "and keep a record of your times after each workout."

"Do I have to? I just don't feel like living swimming 24 hours a day," Don said.

Although coach Haines may have wondered about his new student's attitude, he soon had no doubts about Don's talent. That summer Don tied the 200-meter world record and broke the American record at 440 yards.

Don owed a great deal of his physical ability and competitive drive to his parents. He was born April 30, 1946, in Charlotte, North Carolina. His father, Wendell, had been an honorable mention All-America football player at North Dakota State during the 1930s. His mother, Martha, was a fine swimmer who had doubled for actress Maureen O'Sullivan in Tarzan movies.

The Schollanders moved to Kansas and California before finally settling in Lake Oswego, Oregon, when Don was seven. Don had already begun to swim by then. By the time he was nine he started setting national records in the age-group program. His luck changed, however, when he became 11-years-old. Don got pneumonia and was bedridden for a month.

After his recovery Don moved up to a higher age-group. Because most of the boys were bigger than he, Don suffered loss after loss. He wanted to quit swimming then and there, but his father wouldn't hear of it. "You can quit swimming if you want to,"

Don Schollander heads for a world record in the 400-meter freestyle in the 1964 Olympics.

Mr. Schollander told Don, "but it will be when you're at the top of your age group, not at the bottom."

Finally, when Don was 13, he began to grow. His swimming kept pace. By the next year he had set 11 national age-group records and was beating college boys in the Northwest. Ready for the very best coaching now, Don decided he would get it under Haines at Santa Clara. It was a wise choice.

By the 1964 Olympics Don was nearly fully developed. He stood 5-foot-10½ and weighed 166 pounds—a man despite his boyish face. And he put on a man-sized show at Tokyo. He won his first gold medal at 100 meters with an Olympic-record time of 53.4 seconds. Before he was through he had also set a world record of 4:12.2 at 400 meters and had helped set two more in the 400- and 800-meter freestyle relays. Don became the first swimmer to win four gold medals in a single Olympics.

Schollander was the first swimmer ever to win four gold medals in one Olympics.

The biggest hero of the Olympics, he was mobbed wherever he went in Japan. He attracted people not only with his swimming victories but also with his winning personality. Once, in desperation, he disguised himself in a girl's raincoat and scarf. People recognized him anyway.

When he got home, letters and gifts from around the world poured in by the hundreds. Don received every honor possible in athlete-of-the-year polls. His biggest thrill was being named ahead of one of his boyhood heroes, Johnny Unitas, in a wire-service poll.

Don had his pick of colleges, finally choosing Yale over such swimming powers as Indiana, Southern California and Michigan. "What I like about it," he said after enrolling at the school in New Haven, "is that I'm there on a partial academic scholarship based on need. That means if I don't want to swim a stroke, I don't have to."

But swimming had been too much a part of Don's life for him to dismiss it entirely. He decided to see how long he could stay on top, knowing that swimming was one sport where champions reached their peak early and then faded rapidly.

During the early summer of 1965 Don found out how hard his new task would be. He collapsed from mononucleosis, and was in bed for a month and a half. When he began swimming again in October, the road back was slow.

His first real test came in the National AAU indoor championships in early April 1966. Although he had completely recovered from the effects of the mononucleosis, now Don was weak from a recent flu attack. On the first day of the meet he failed to qualify for the finals of the 500-yard freestyle. It was the first time that he had failed to qualify for a major event in many years. The next day he won his old reliable, the 200, but Don knew that wasn't enough to prove he was still the world's best swimmer.

Schollander's do-or-die moment came in late August at the AAU outdoor championships. The first event was the 400. In the preliminary John Nelson broke the world record Don had set in the Olympics. But in the finals it was all Schollander, with Don recapturing the record with a time of 4:11.6.

"I could have won a lot of money betting on you today," George Haines told Don afterward. "A lot of coaches didn't give you much of a chance."

The next day Don lowered his own world

record in the 200 to 1:56.2. He followed that up by setting a meet record in the 100, and then swam anchor legs on the winning 400- and 800-meter relay teams. Altogether Don collected five gold medals at the meet and was easily voted the most outstanding swimmer.

Don returned to Yale in the fall, trying as always to lead a full and normal life. He swam an hour and a half a day, studied hard enough to get a B average as an economics major, and still had time to belong to several organizations.

Nevertheless, he also began to realize the pressure of trying to keep his top ranking in swimming. "I'm not so much swimming to win now, as not to lose," he said. "It's human nature to root for the underdog."

Anyone who rooted against Schollander was still fighting a losing battle. Don successfully defended his 100- and 200-meter titles at the 1967 outdoor AAUs, and once again lowered his world record in the 200 meters.

Don also set a new swimming goal. He wanted to become the first American male swimmer since Johnny Weissmuller to win gold medals in two Olympics. Weissmuller had done it back in 1924 and 1928.

Although coach Haines thought Don had a very good chance to attain his goal, he made a suggestion that he figured would help. Not notebooks this time—just the opposite. He wanted Don to put aside his books for a semester in 1968 and devote all his time to preparing for the Games in Mexico. Haines knew that Yale's tough academic standards would cut down Don's training time to about half of what it should be. He also knew Don was a good enough student to resume his studies after the Olympics were over.

But again Don balked at Haines' advice. This time, however, teacher may have

known best. At the Olympic trials in August, Don had his worst day in five years. He finished fifth in the 100-meter freestyle. That meant he was ineligible to compete for the United States in either the 100 meters or the 400-meter relay. Fortunately, Don was stronger than ever in his favorite race, the 200 meters. He broke his own world record with a clocking of 1:54.3, and earned a spot on the U. S. team in that event, and in the 800-meter relay.

At the Olympics, Don again tasted defeat along with victory. The 800-meter relay team won easily, giving Don his fifth Olympic gold medal. But he lost the 200 to Michael Wenden of Australia. Wenden's time of 1:55.2 was an Olympic record, yet .9 off Schollander's best.

If Don was at all disappointed, he didn't show it. At the ripe old age of 22, his swimming career was over, and he was glad. He recalled the funny feeling he had had at the Pan American Games the previous summer, seeing so many fresh-faced 16-year-olds in the water. "I felt a little like an old man," Don said. "I've lasted through two generations of swimmers and I'm tired."

Don's career didn't end exactly as he had planned, yet he still had been on top for six years. No other American swimmer in the modern era had ever held on for more than two years.

Don achieved his goals on his own terms. He always insisted that there was more to life than swimming, and he considered himself more than just a swimmer. "I'm a *person* who happens to swim," he said over and over. To Don, the distinction was important. That is why he refused to keep records of his times, or drop out of Yale for a semester.

Most athletes couldn't think the way Schollander did and still become a world champion. Don got away with it because his

Trying out for the Olympic team in 1968, Don begins the 200-meter freestyle. He set a new world record of 1:54.2.

stroke in the water was flawless, and because he was a smart and tough competitor. "When Don is ready to race, he knows it," Yale coach Phil Moriarty said in 1968. "He sets dozens of tiny personal standards for himself. When they're all met, he's up."

Finally, the moment came—that moment when he climbed out of the pool for the last time. A few minutes later he was sitting in the stands surrounding the Mexico City pool. Someone came over and asked Don what he was going to do now. He replied that he hoped to finish at Yale the next year and then go to work for a financial firm. As for swimming, he said, all that was left was to write a book—"about my philosophy of swimming, what made me go, that sort of thing."

No one in the history of the sport was more entitled to write such a book. For the generations of swimmers to follow, it would be required reading.

O. J. SIMPSON

When O. J. Simpson entered the University of Southern California in January 1967, he seemed too good to be true. He was big: 6-foot-2, 205 pounds. He was fast: 100-yard dash in 9.4. And he was a one-man touchdown machine: 54 touchdowns in two years of junior college, a national record.

O. J. entered Southern Cal in the spring semester but he didn't spend much time at spring football practice. He was too busy with the track team. But football coach John McKay did notice one disturbing thing about O. J.'s ball carrying. When Simpson ran into the line, he tended to fumble. McKay wasn't terribly upset, because he knew O. J. hadn't had much experience carrying the ball inside. In junior college, O. J. had been used as a flanker and an outside runner. Still, McKay had to solve the problem.

McKay's solution was simple. He devised a drill in which two big linemen confronted O. J. with five-foot-high tackling dummies. O. J. had to run between them, take the jolt they gave him and keep on going. Then, about two yards downfield, was another lineman with a tackling dummy. O. J. had to try to elude this "tackler" and turn on his speed. Further downfield, other players threw heavy air bags at O. J.'s feet and knees. The point of the whole drill was to teach O. J. to hit, elude, make his moves in the open field, and still hold on to the ball.

Gradually O. J. began to cut down his fumbling. Coach McKay was impressed even more with O. J.'s determination during the rough drill. "He kept at it and at it," McKay said, looking back the next year. "It was as if he were saying, 'This is where I am going to make my name.' "

In his very first play for USC against

O. J. Simpson takes the ball for the University of Southern California.

Washington State, O. J. caught a swing pass and gained 15 yards. By the time he had run his last play, he had scored 36 touchdowns and broken many major-college rushing records. And his team was a winner. In his two years, USC won 19 games, lost just two and tied one. He led the team to the national championship in 1967 and into the Rose Bowl twice.

O. J. was rewarded both with honors and money. He was a consensus All-America in '67 and '68 and won the 1968 Heisman Trophy which is given each year to the outstanding college football player in the country. In a 1969 poll of the experts to determine the greatest college players of football's first century, O. J. was the top running back in 40 years, ranking behind Red Grange and Jim Thorpe. When his college career was over, O. J. became a highly paid representative of a major automobile company and he was guaranteed an estimated $400,-000 to sign with the Buffalo Bills of the American Football League.

Simpson had many talents. Coach McKay called him, "the fastest man of his size ever to play the game." O. J. also had great peripheral vision. "Most backs are 'blinders,'" McKay explained. "They see what's in front, but can't see what's at the side. O. J. is the only man I've known who can come back to the huddle and tell who made the key blocks."

O. J. had amazing skill at slipping past would-be tacklers. Films showed he could change directions in a 24th of a second while running at full speed. He was big enough to run over opponents, but he usually did this only as a last resort.

"If I know I can't get away, then I'll pick one guy and just run straight into him," O. J. said. "After you smash into him you look for his number. Then later in the game, if you can, you run at him again. You can just see the guy tighten up, flat-footed and tense, waiting for you to make the first move. That's when you have him."

Simpson also had one other asset that made him stick in people's minds: his colorful name. When Southern Cal played Michigan State, State's coach Duffy Daugherty jokingly called Simpson "Orange Juice," which is what O. J. stands for in a restau-rant. For Simpson, O. J. really stands for Orenthal James. According to Simpson, he was named by an aunt who gave her own children more common names—Stewart, Stanley and Pam.

O. J. grew up in a black neighborhood of San Francisco called Portrero Hills. He and his brother and two sisters were raised by their mother, a hospital worker. Her dream for O. J. was that someday he would become a big sports star like his cousin, Ernie Banks of the Chicago Cubs.

Simpson was a great athlete right from the start, but he also got into trouble with police and school officials. In junior high he ran with a gang that would throw rocks at buses, pull fire alarms and get into fights with other gangs. Later on he came close to being a high-school dropout.

"School didn't mean much to us then," O. J. has said. "We were always getting hauled into the dean's office for cutting classes, smoking, playing with dice. If it hadn't been for football, I guess we would have just quit coming to school."

O. J. began to straighten out when he and his friends discovered the Booker T. Washington Community Center. They formed a social club there, calling themselves The Superiors. O. J., always a leader, was its president. He also started dating pretty Marguerite Whitley, the girl he later married.

O. J. was an all-city running back his senior year at Galileo High School. But unlike other good high school players, O. J. was not recruited by a major college. His grades were too low to meet senior college entrance requirements. He worked for a year and then enrolled at the City College of San Francisco. He averaged 9.9 yards a carry as a freshman and scored 26 touchdowns.

After his first year of college, Arizona State University and the University of Utah were eager to admit O. J. But the Uni-

Against UCLA in 1967, Simpson shoots through the defense to score on a 13-yard run. Late in the game he scored again, leading USC to a 21–20 victory.

versity of Southern California, his first choice, still required more junior college credits. So O. J. went back to City College for another year and scored 28 more touchdowns during his second season. He entered USC for the spring term of 1967.

During the spring, O. J. was a member of the USC relay team which set a world record in the 440-yard relay. That fall he began setting records of his own on the football field.

In a game early in 1967, O. J. showed his talent. USC was trailing Notre Dame 7–0, in the third period. The Trojans took the ball on their own 18 yard line. O. J. carried on seven straight plays, cutting through the big Notre Dame line and taking USC 70 yards. Finally, on fourth down from the one yard line, he somersaulted into the end zone. The point-after tied the game at 7–7.

Later in the quarter USC had a third-down situation on Notre Dame's 36. Simpson took a pass from quarterback Steve Sogge and raced down the sideline for another score. O. J. later scored a third touchdown and Southern Cal won easily, 24–7.

O. J. hurt his foot in the game against Oregon and missed the next game. He returned the next week stronger than ever. He gained 188 yards in the mud against Oregon State, although USC suffered its only loss of the year, 3–0.

In the last game of the regular season, Southern Cal played its crosstown rival, UCLA, in the Los Angeles Coliseum. The winner would become champion of the Pacific Eight Conference and receive an invitation to the Rose Bowl. If USC lost, it would also lose its chance to be the Number One team in college football.

In his first year with the Buffalo Bills, Simpson tries to thread his way through the New York Jets defenses.

The game also matched the two leading candidates for the Heisman Trophy—O. J. and UCLA's quarterback Gary Beban. Many players would have been nervous and apprehensive. But O. J. truly looked forward to the clash. "I always play better in pressure games," he said. "That's what it's all about, isn't it?"

Late in the game, Southern Cal had the ball on its own 36. O. J. had been carrying all afternoon. In the huddle, USC quarterback Steve Sogge called a play that would give O. J. a rest. But at the line of scrimmage Sogge saw a UCLA player out of position and called an "audible"—a new play that would take advantage of UCLA's mistake. It was a hand-off to O. J.

"Oh, he's crazy," thought O. J.

Sogge knew what he was doing. O. J. took the hand-off, bolted off left tackle, cut toward the sideline, then swerved back across the field for a 64-yard touchdown. The touchdown and the extra point gave Southern Cal the victory, 21–20.

O. J. had run for 177 yards against UCLA, giving him a total of 1415 for the year, the highest in the nation. But the Heisman Trophy went to Gary Beban, UCLA's great quarterback.

Simpson wasted no time getting 1968 off on the right foot. On New Year's Day, in the Rose Bowl, he scored the only two touchdowns of the entire game. They came on two-yard and eight-yard runs, and USC beat Indiana, 14–3.

O. J. carried the ball often as a junior, but during his senior year he carried it even more. In the first game, against Minnesota, he carried 39 times for 236 yards, caught six passes, and scored four touchdowns. Twice during that season O. J. carried the ball 47 times in a game.

People thought he was tireless, but if they only knew! The 24 hours after a game were torture for O. J. "I'd sit up half the night watching TV, because I didn't want to go to bed," O. J. said at the end of the season. "Because when I'd get in bed, I couldn't sleep. Part of it was mental tension. And a lot was just physical pain. Every way I'd turn, every place I'd lie, I'd hurt. The next day would be awful."

During the 1968 season, O. J. carried the ball 355 times and set a major-college rushing record of 1709 yards. And he won his Heisman Trophy, gaining 855 of the 1042 first-place votes.

Simpson's last game for USC was the 1969 Rose Bowl game against Ohio State. He gained 171 yards, including an 80-yard touchdown run, and he caught eight passes. But even his fine performance wasn't enough for USC: they lost to a strong Ohio State team, 27–16.

When the professional teams began to draft college players, Simpson hoped he'd be taken by a West Coast team. But Buffalo had first pick and they picked O. J. After long negotiations with Buffalo, he finally signed on August 9, after the team was in training, for a guarantee of $400,000.

There could have been some friction between O. J. and his new teammates: he came to camp late and was being paid more as a rookie than any veteran on the team. But he won them over quickly with his tact and sense of humor. He also won them over as a football player. He gained nearly 700 yards in his first season, and ranked among the top five rushers in the league even though the Bills were a team that often had to play catch-up football, which meant more passing and less running. O. J.'s teammates knew exactly what he had gone through to get those yards. There seemed to be little doubt that O. J.'s determination and pride would make him as unforgettable in pro ball as he had been in college.

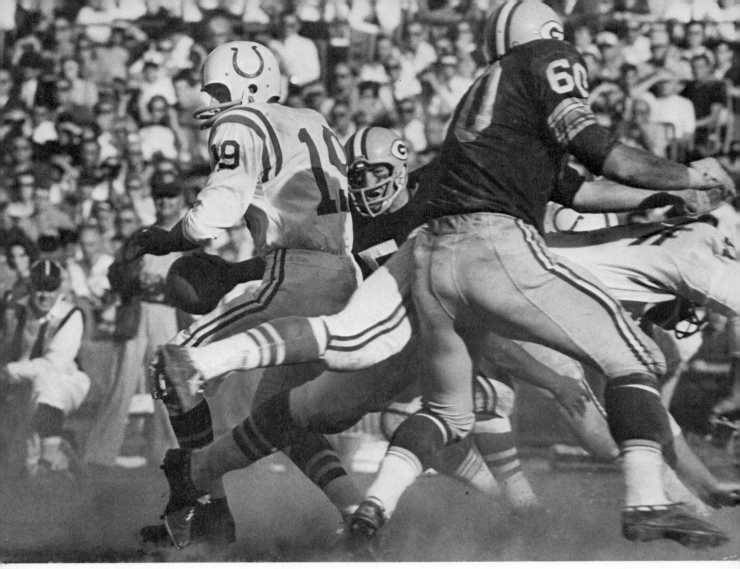

Working under the pressure of Green Bay's pass rush, Johnny Unitas (19) drops back to pass for Baltimore.

JOHNNY UNITAS

There were two and a half minutes left to play. The powerful Green Bay Packers were leading the Baltimore Colts, 10–0, and a Packer victory seemed certain on this cool and windy day in 1967 at Baltimore's Memorial Stadium. The 60,000 Colt fans were standing but silent, with defeat only 150 seconds away.

The Colts had the ball on their 32-yard line. Their quarterback, Johnny Unitas, scanned the Packer defense. He leaned over the center, barking out signals. He took the snap, faded back and threw a pass. Com-

plete. He threw again, and again. Six plays later, from the Packer 10, he lobbed the ball into the end zone where Alex Hawkins caught it for a touchdown.

But the Colts' Lou Michaels missed the kick for the extra point. With the score 10–6 against them, the Colts needed another touchdown to win. And now there were only 120 seconds left to play.

The Colts lined up for an on-side kickoff. The ball bounced off a Green Bay leg and the Colts recovered the ball on the Green Bay 34. With 60,000 Baltimore fans screeching for Johnny U. to work another Unitas miracle, Johnny led the Colt offense onto the field.

Three plays gained only four yards. On fourth and sixth, the Packer defense lined up to defend against the pass. On the snap the Packer linemen charged in. Unitas dashed right by them, carrying the ball himself. He was running for daylight. He got past the line of scrimmage but then a Packer linebacker swiped him from the side and down he went. He bounced up quickly, looking toward the sideline yardsticks.

First down! He'd made it with a yard to spare.

Johnny looked at the clock. Ninety seconds remaining. From the Packer 23, he dropped back into his cup of blockers. He saw Colt flanker Willie Richardson angling toward the goal posts, just ahead of Packer defender Herb Adderley. Johnny tossed a high, arching pass. Adderley leaped for the ball, and missed it. Richardson brought it down on his fingertips at the 3 and tumbled into the end zone for the touchdown. The Colts had won the game, 13–10.

Later in the Colt clubhouse Alex Hawkins said to somebody: "How can you ever give up when you have Unitas going for you?"

All through the 1960s the Colts had Johnny U. going for them and time after time he won games that were seemingly lost. In 1964 the Colts won the NFL western title but were beaten by the Browns for the NFL championship. In 1968 they won the NFL championship, though Unitas was on the sideline most of the year with an aching arm. With Unitas at quarterback, every Colt team had won more than half its games.

For most of the decade Johnny was bothered by arm injuries that made him wince when he threw. In his stoic way, he said, "It will always hurt and there is nothing I can do about it except forget about it hurting and throw."

His throwing set so many league and team records it would require a column of type to list them all: most passes attempted in a career, most passes completed in a career, most yardage gained by passing, the most touchdown passes thrown during a career. One of his records may stand for decades: beginning in 1956 he threw touchdown passes in 47 consecutive games, breaking the old record of 22. No quarterback of the 1960s came within 20 games of equaling that record.

Curiously, pro football once rejected Johnny Unitas. In the summer of 1955, the Pittsburgh Steelers had seen him try out at their summer camp. "Too small, not good enough," said the Steeler coaches. Johnny hitchhiked home and got a job on a construction crew, playing sandlot football for $6 a game to keep in shape. "I know I can make it in pro ball," he told his wife. "I just need the chance."

Ever since grade school in Pittsburgh, Johnny had wanted to play pro football. While he hauled buckets of coal up the stairs of Pittsburgh tenements, he dreamed about playing for the Pittsburgh Steelers and throwing touchdown passes in Forbes Field. His father died in 1937 when Johnny was 4. At 9, Johnny was helping his mother run the coal-delivery business his father had owned. At St. Justin High he was a flashy quarterback and he yearned to go to Notre Dame. A Notre Dame coach gave him a tryout but shook his head when he saw Johnny's skinny 165-pound frame, and said, "Too small."

Johnny went to the University of Louisville where he dazzled football fans with his gambler's daring. Once, with the ball on his 40, fourth down and two yards to go, he called for a pass. He threw the ball over the bunched-up defense for a 60-yard touch-down.

The Steelers drafted him, but then shattered his dream by cutting him from the squad. But he kept himself ready for the chance he knew would come. The chance came in 1956 when the Colts invited Johnny to their training camp. Halfway through the season the Colts' first-string quarterback was hurt in a game against the Bears. Unitas dashed into the game. He stepped back to pass, threw the ball, and the Bears intercepted. The Colts lost, 58–27.

A calm, unruffled person even as a rookie, Johnny said, "I know I have got to get one more chance. I am the only quarterback they have."

The next week he passed the Colts to vic-tory. On the last day of that 1956 season he displayed what would become a Unitas specialty. With 15 seconds to go he threw a 53-yard touchdown pass to beat the Red-skins.

In 1958 he showed millions of TV viewers an example of his daring in what has been called "the greatest football game ever played." It was the Colts against the Giants for the NFL championship. With 1:56 left in the game, the Colts were losing 17–14 and took possession on their own 14. Amid the roar of some 60,000 people in Yankee Stadium, Unitas calmly threw passes that shot through the Giant defense into the hands of Colt receivers. The Colts swept to the Giant 13, then kicked a field goal to tie the game, 17–17, and send it into

Calm and poised, Unitas throws to his receiver. He was a daring signal-caller and passer.

sudden-death overtime: the first team to score would be the winner.

In the overtime Unitas moved the Colts to a first down on the Giant 8. Coach Weeb Ewbank sent in an order: run three times and if you don't score, kick a field goal.

On first down Unitas ran the ball into the line. As the play unfolded for a short gain, Unitas noticed a hole in the Giant defense. To take advantage of the hole, he disobeyed the coach and called for a pass. He threw to end Jim Mutscheller, who caught the ball over his shoulder and fell out of bounds at the Giant 1. On the next play fullback Alan Ameche plunged into the end zone for a 23–17 victory and the NFL title.

After the game the calm Unitas was asked: "Why did you risk a pass when a field goal would have won for you? The pass could have been intercepted."

Right then Unitas established himself as the fearless gambler. "When you know what you are doing," he said grimly, "they're not intercepted."

Nor were too many of his passes intercepted during the next dozen years. He'd become a husky 200-pound six-footer, but he was plagued by sore fingers and an aching right elbow that took some of the zip out of his passes during the last years of his career. In one game against the Bears he displayed the physical courage that made him even more dangerous when he was hurting. The Colts were losing, 20–17, with less than two minutes to play. Unitas ran back to pass. Two big Bear linemen, Bill George and Doug Atkins, swarmed on Johnny and smashed him to the grass.

He got up slowly, blood running out of his nose and mouth. He staggered to the bench, where a trainer stuffed cotton wadding up Johnny's nostrils and pasted bandages across his mouth to stop the bleeding. Johnny went back into the game.

Unitas watches glumly from the sidelines as the Colts lose to the Jets in the 1969 Super Bowl.

There were 25 seconds remaining, the ball on the Bear 40. Again he ran back to pass. In charged George and Atkins. Johnny ducked under their lashing fists, giving his receiver, the speedy Lenny Moore, time to get ahead of his man. He faked to throw once, then again, ignoring the huge Bears battling to get at him. He saw Moore open daylight between himself and his man. Only then did he throw.

The ball soared some 45 yards downfield, Moore catching it on the goal line and skidding into the end zone. Touchdown with 17 seconds to play. The Colts were winners, 24-20.

"Only a perfect play could have saved them," a Bear said in the loser's clubhouse. "And Unitas came up with the perfect play."

And why not? With that courage and daring and arm, he was the perfect quarterback.

DICK WEBER

The high school athletic director called Dick Weber into his office and told him he had some unpleasant news. The school was going to bar Dick from any scholastic sports. Dick was shocked and upset. He had been all set to try and earn his letter in baseball, a sport he loved.

"Why am I being barred?" Dick finally asked.

Because he was a pro, said the director.

Now Dick's shock turned to anger. The school had based its decision on Dick's meager winnings in a bowling league. "I'd bowled in a league where you paid $1.55 to roll three games," Dick explained years later. "The games cost 30 cents each, and the league put the other 65 cents in the fund. At the end of the season I got about $20 in prize money. But I'd paid $40 into the kitty."

The athletic director didn't realize it at the time, but his action was going to change Dick Weber's entire life—for the better. Dick got so angry that he decided he'd give up baseball and all other sports entirely, except for bowling. And then he set out to be the best bowler possible.

It took many years of hard work for Dick

Dick Weber rolls the ball during tournament play.

to make it big, but he finally made it in 1961 when he was named the Professional Bowler of the Year. He repeated the next year and won the honor a third time in 1965. By the end of the '60s, he had a career average of more than 200 pins per game and there wasn't a major tournament he hadn't won.

Dick Weber had been born in Indianapolis, Indiana, on December 23, 1929, and was rolling a bowling ball almost before he could lift it. One night, when he was seven, he went to the bowling alley with his father. Dick's father wasn't doing very well that night, and his teammates suggested he might as well sit down and let little Dick finish out the game.

Dick rolled his first ball into the gutter, but then he got most of the pins on the next ball and finally picked up a spare. A sportswriter at the alley that night typed out a story about Dick. He wrote, jokingly, that this might be the debut of a coming champ. Little did he know.

When Dick was ten he became a pinboy doing the work that is usually done today by automatic pinsetters. He earned five cents a line. He also joined a pinboys' league. Later he found out that if he worked as a porter around the alleys, he sometimes would be asked to fill in for a missing player in the adult leagues. But after a while his father began to disapprove, fearing Dick would become an alley bum.

During the daytime Dick played basketball and baseball, and he was good at both. But he was too small to go far in basketball; even as an adult he would grow to only 5-foot-9, 125 pounds. And his dreams of becoming a major-league shortstop were ended by the athletic director's ruling. So Dick continued to get in all the bowling he could, despite his father's warnings.

After graduation Dick began working full-time in a bowling alley. One of his co-workers was a pretty cashier named Juanita. They were married in 1948, three months after their first date. Dick had only $20 in the bank, and their combined salaries were only $80 a week. To make ends meet, Dick went to work as a mail clerk at the post office.

By 1953 Dick was probably the best bowler in Indiana, and was earning around $2,000 a year from small tournaments. In 1955 he got his first big break. He finished 11th in the important All Star tournament in Chicago. Just as he was packing his gear to go home, a voice said to him, "Can I talk to you a minute, Dick?"

Weber looked up. It was Don Carter, one of the world's greatest bowlers. "Sure," Dick said, awed by the well-known Carter.

"Don McLaren is leaving the Budweisers to take a job out of town," Carter said. "We're looking for somebody to take his place on the team. From what I saw of your bowling here, I'd say that you can do the job. It would mean moving to St. Louis. But Budweiser will pay you a salary of $3,600 a year, and you'll have a chance to pick up more in tournament winnings."

Dick didn't have to think twice about the opportunity. Besides Carter and McLaren, the Budweiser team had Ray Bluth, Pat Patterson and Billy Welu. It was the greatest bowling team ever assembled, as powerful and successful as the New York Yankees of Ruth and Gehrig.

Weber proved to be an important addition and helped the team win four national titles between 1955 and 1960. Dick also was teaming up with Ray Bluth in doubles and doing very well. They won the national title in '56, '60 and '61.

The Budweiser team finally was disbanded in December 1960 because of an unusual problem. They had become "too good." They were in such demand that they

Weber demonstrates his bowling technique outside of New York's Madison Square Garden.

offended many bowling houses by not having the time to go there and give exhibitions. Rather than create ill will, they felt it was wiser to go their separate ways.

For Dick, it seemed to be the push he needed to establish himself on his own. In 1961 he became almost unbeatable, winning tournament after tournament all over the country. In one stretch he won five out of

six, and ten altogether on the tour. No one else won more than one. "I never saw anybody bowl like that before," said Billy Welu. "The guy was fantastic."

There was, however, still one nagging doubt in the back of Dick's mind. He had never yet won one of the long, rugged tournaments, like the All Star. The big tournaments stretch over several weeks and Dick wondered if his small build might keep him from having the stamina of the bigger bowlers.

He entered the 1961-62 All Star with the feeling that if he ever was going to win it, now was the time. With three games to go in the finals, Dick trailed the leader, Roy Lown, by a slight margin. Suddenly, Dick lost his touch. He was inconsistent in the first game, and even worse in the second.

"I'd been terribly nervous," Dick would recall later, "but now I was just plain mad at myself. I was racking my brains trying to figure out what I was doing wrong. Should I slow the ball down or speed it up? Finally in the last frame of that second game I said what the heck and just sort of tossed the ball in anger. I got a strike and I felt better right away. I was loosened up and my timing came back."

Dick was 21 pins behind going into the last game, but he started chopping away at Lown's lead. By the end of the game Lown had 213 and Weber 248. Dick won the match by 15 pins and collected the tournament's $15,000 first prize.

Weber went on to win a total of $53,000 in tournament play for 1962. From then on his fortune was made. Endorsements, exhibitions and investments took his earnings into the $100,000 bracket. It was a long way from his $3,700-a-year post office job.

In 1965 Dick reached his peak, topping even his '61 and '62 seasons. He won the All Star for the third time in four years; averaged 212 for over two thousand games, and again led the money-winners with around $50,000. His most exciting moment came in the Houston Open when he rolled three perfect 300-games in two days, giving him 15 for his career.

In the latter half of the 1960s Dick declined a bit. He was approaching his 40s and the young bowlers coming up were bet-

Weber accepts his trophy after winning the All Star Bowling Tournament in 1963.

ter than ever. But he still never strayed very far from the top, and he remained as respected as anyone in the game. In early 1970, in the voting for election to the bowling Hall of Fame, Dick was second only to Don Carter. Dick had no regrets about losing out to the older master. He knew his time would come on the next ballot.

With no time left on the clock, Jerry West's 55-foot shot is in the basket, tying the third game of the 1970 NBA playoff. West (far right) has just crossed the middle line.

JERRY WEST

It was the third game of a best-of-seven series. At stake was the 1970 championship of the National Basketball Association. The two teams were the Los Angeles Lakers, winners of the Western Division, and the New York Knicks, champions of the East. Each team had won one game.

The Lakers held a 56–42 lead at halftime. But the Knicks came back strong in the third period. Then, with three seconds left in the game and the score tied, 100 apiece, Dave DeBusschere of New York hit an off-balance shot from 20 feet. The game seemed over, with not enough time remaining for the Lakers even to bring the ball all the way downcourt.

The in-bounds pass went to the Lakers' superstar guard, Jerry West. Jerry had jammed his left thumb in the first half, but he had refused to come out and had played every minute of the game. As usual he was leading the Lakers in scoring, just as he had led the entire NBA in scoring during the regular season.

Now, as Jerry dribbled the ball past a Knick, he looked up at the clock hanging over the basket down at the other end of the court. One second remained. He still was 15 feet from midcourt, but he had no choice except to shoot. Summoning all his strength, he pushed the ball one-handed in the general direction of the basket. "I had no idea what was going to happen to it," he said in the locker room later.

No one else could have predicted what happened either. Incredibly, the ball hit the back of the rim and dropped straight through the net. It had gone 55 feet, making it one of the longest and most dramatic shots in basketball history. It was also one more spectacular example of why Jerry West, in his long career with the Lakers, had come to be known as "Mr. Clutch." When the Lakers needed a crucial basket, Jerry seldom failed them. It was estimated that he had won more basketball games in the final seconds than any player ever.

Unfortunately, the Lakers lost the game to the Knicks in overtime, 111–108. But this too had become typical of the Jerry West story. Despite Jerry's greatness, the Lakers always seemed to fall inches short of their goal. In Jerry's first ten seasons—1960–61 through 1969–70—the Lakers played in the NBA playoffs eight times. Yet the Lakers never won once. It was a frustration that gnawed deeply at West. "There are many reasons for playing this game," he has said, "but winning is the best one."

Because Jerry's team never won the title, it took time for many fans to appreciate him fully. The moment finally came in the 1969 playoff finals against the Boston Celtics. By the end of that seven-game series, most people were calling him the greatest all-round player in the game. Certainly there was no greater competitor.

West started the series by scoring 53 points, with Los Angeles winning, 120–118. The Lakers won the second game, too, with Jerry hitting for 41. His long jump shot, from every angle, was never deadlier. The Celtics won the next two games in Boston. Jerry scored 40 points in the second of the two, including a jumper with 20 seconds remaining to give the Lakers a one-point lead. But the Lakers lost the game anyway.

In game No. 5 the Lakers won behind Jerry's 39 points. But the injury jinx, which had plagued him ever since he came to the NBA, struck again. He pulled a hamstring muscle in his leg. Normally this would mean a two-day layoff, but West insisted that as long as he could stand up, he would play. And he did play the next game, despite a heavy bandage, pain and loss of mobility, and he scored 26 points. But the Lakers lost again, to send the series back to Los Angeles for the seventh and deciding game.

With nine minutes left in the final game, the Lakers didn't seem to stand a chance. They trailed, 100–83. Then West went to work, a man who was sick and tired of playing on the losing side in the big game. He was still limping, yet he drove all over the court, shooting with radar-like accuracy, then falling back on defense to try and get the ball back. Of Los Angeles' next 19 points, Jerry scored 14. By the end of the game Jerry had 42 points, 13 rebounds and 12 assists. But it still wasn't enough. The Celtics won the game, and the championship, by two points, 108–106.

In the dressing room later, Jerry was informed that he had won a Dodge Charger from *Sport* Magazine as the Most Valuable Player in the series. Such awards seldom go to players on losing teams. Jerry appreciated the award and the many compliments but they didn't relieve the awful ache of losing the title once again. Sitting there in the dressing room, his sore leg propped up on a chair, he said, "I guess it just isn't meant to be." Then he went into the shower and cried.

Jerry West had begun preparing for a basketball career from the time he was able to lift the ball. He was born on May 28, 1938, in Cheylan, West Virginia, and by the time he was in grade school he and the ball seldom parted company. Once, when he was ten, he and a friend played in the rain. Jerry came into the house to change into clean shoes three times. The third time was just too much for Jerry's mother. "I bent him over my knee and gave him a good paddling," she has said. "But the next day he was right back out there again."

Jerry went to East Bank High School and led his team to the state championship. There wasn't much doubt that he'd go on to West Virginia University. The WVU coach, Fred Schaus, had been scouting Jerry since he was a sophomore, and Jerry himself wanted to play in his home state.

West became a three-time All-America at WVU, and led the team to the NCAA finals in 1959, his junior year. That championship game was an omen of what was to come in the pros. While Jerry was high scorer with 28 points and was voted the Most Valuable Player in the tournament, WVU lost the title to California, by one point.

Jerry's heroics in high school and college made him a hero in West Virginia. Once when he was in college he was invited to visit the governor. He went up to the receptionist and said, "I'm Jerry West. I have an appointment with the governor."

"You don't have to tell me who you are," said the receptionist. "You're better known than the governor."

In the summer of 1960, shortly after graduation, Jerry was named a co-captain of the U. S. Olympic team, along with Oscar Robertson. It was perhaps the greatest basketball team in Olympic history. No country came closer than 24 points of the Americans.

West joined the Lakers that fall, happy to be reunited with his college coach, Fred Schaus, who became coach of the Lakers. Jerry started fast. He brought the ball upcourt, called the plays, played fine defense and, in the words of Schaus, "had a great year for a first-year man."

Yet Jerry was dissatisfied. "I was awkward," he said. "I had little confidence. I didn't drive enough. I wasn't moving to my left." So he went up to the summer camp which he helped run, and he worked on his problems. He would line up several of the 12- and 13-year-old campers and try to maneuver through all of them. He also spent hours practicing foul shots.

The results were noticeable. He raised his scoring average from 17.6 to 30.8. But now another problem began to emerge: Jerry seemed injury prone. In a brief stretch early in the 1961 season Jerry sprained his right ankle three separate times, and took a fearful battering under the basket from larger, heavier opponents. Writer Arnold Hano considered Jerry's frail-looking 6-foot-3, 175-pound frame, and his crooked nose which had been broken four times in basketball. Then Hano suggested that West might not last five more years in the league.

But Hano was wrong. He had misjudged Jerry's pride, his ability to adjust and his overall toughness. Not that things got any easier physically for Jerry. By the end of the 1960s he had broken his nose four or five more times, and had damage done to just about every area of his body. Though he practically had to be strapped in bed to keep him out of a game, he still missed 128 games in his first nine seasons.

When Jerry was out of the lineup, the Lakers suffered. They missed his leadership and his unselfish play. They missed his consistently high scoring: in his first ten years his overall average was close to 28 points a game. Most of all, they missed his clutch play.

"He's a killer," said an opposing coach. "Forget my name, because I don't want to offend my own players, but I have to admit this guy is the greatest clutch player ever, just unbelievable. In the last few minutes of close games, I tell my guys that if you let him get the ball, you might as well go home."

It is impossible to recount all the games Jerry won in the closing seconds, but one of the more memorable came in the third game of the final playoffs in 1962. Boston

West goes up for a shot against the Cincinnati Royals.

West rests on the bench during a game.

led the Lakers, 115–111, with time running out. West hit on a jump shot. After Boston missed a shot, West was fouled trying to shoot another jumper. He sank both free throws to tie the score. After Boston called time out, the Celtics took the ball in-bounds at midcourt. Three seconds were left when Sam Jones tried to pass in to Bob Cousy. West leaped forward, stole the ball, drove toward the basket and laid it up as the buzzer went off.

What was it that made Jerry West so effective in the clutch? Even Jerry didn't know for sure. "Maybe the challenge stimulates me," he said. "I know there are good players in this league who don't want the ball in the tight situations. But I want the ball, I know I can do something with it. Because I've done it before. Not always—no one does it always. But often enough. And I'm proud of it."

Early in the 1969–70 season Jerry reflected both on that season and on his long career. He was on his way to another 30-plus scoring average, but it would not be an easy year. Wilt Chamberlain missed most of the season with a knee injury; Elgin Baylor was out at times, too, leaving Jerry with a huge burden. Meanwhile, Jerry himself was getting his lumps as usual. One night he crashed to the floor head first and required ten stitches in his forehead. He admitted he never felt so tired and talked about retiring. "If I wind up having a good year," he said, "I don't know if I'd take a chance on another one, on having a bad one."

West's performances in the 1970 playoffs made it hard to believe that he was thinking about retirement. Besides his 55-footer, he sparked the Lakers' victories in the second and fourth games. In the second game he sank two free throws with 45 seconds left to win the game, 105–103. In the fourth, he started slowly, but wound up with 38 points as the Lakers won in overtime. But once again they lost the championship series.

Retirement at that point was not a pleasant thought for West. "When I have to say that I'm not gonna play anymore," he said, "it'll be the hardest thing I'll ever have to do in my life. It'll kill me. I don't look forward to it."

Neither did anyone else, not even the teams that Jerry had beaten in the closing seconds of a tight ball game. They knew that when Jerry West left pro basketball, something special would be missing.

MAURY WILLS

The big crowd watched as the scoreboard flashed all of Maury Wills' records and accomplishments on this night in August, 1969, at Los Angeles' Dodger Stadium. Then an announcer's voice boomed over the rising roar of some 20,000 people: "And now there he is, at shortstop, one of the all-time great Dodger heroes . . . Maury Wills."

Wills, standing at shortstop, took a step forward. The cheers cascaded down upon him, all these fans pouring out a tribute to the greatest base-stealer of his time. After a minute the umpire indicated that the next batter, the Braves' Hank Aaron, should step in. But the roaring rose higher and Aaron stepped out.

For a little more than four minutes they cheered. "I tipped my hat, I blew kisses, but they wouldn't stop," Maury said later. "I thought it would never stop and I began to break out in a sweat, all those people cheering for me. It was the greatest thrill of all my years in baseball."

Few ballplayers have ever given baseball more thrills than Maury Morning Wills. Time and again he danced off first base, arms spread like airplane wings. He stretched his lead, the crowd roaring "Go . . . go . . . go." And suddenly he went, cleats kicking up dirt, streaking for second. In he slid, the infielder grabbing the throw from the catcher and stabbing his glove into the

Maury Wills leads off first (left), watching the pitcher intently. Then, at exactly the right instant he breaks for second base (right).

flying dust. Nearly always the umpire stretched his arms wide—*safe!*—and Maury Wills had stolen another base.

In 1962 he stole 104 bases, breaking Ty Cobb's record of 96, a 47-year-old record that had seemed too formidable ever to be broken. Some whole teams do not steal so many bases in a season. For six seasons in a row, from 1960 to 1965, Wills led the National League in stolen bases—also a record.

He stole bases with a marvelous mixture of speed, instinct and cunning. It is a baseball axiom that you steal a base from the pitcher, not from the catcher, by getting such a big head-start that not even the strongest-armed catcher can throw you out. No one ever got better jumps off pitchers than Maury Wills and no one ever studied pitchers harder to know how to get those jumps.

"Some pitchers lean toward home when they are going to throw to first," he once said. When he saw them leaning toward home, Wills stayed close to first, expecting a throw. When they weren't leaning toward home, Wills knew they would be pitching the ball to the plate and he took off for second base.

"Other pitchers kick high when they're going to throw toward home," he said. "They should slide their foot a little instead of kicking high. That gives them a chance to go to first or home with the ball. But if they do that, then they won't be as effective in their pitching."

Wills studied pitchers from the dugout, from the on-deck circle, from the batter's box. He timed how long they would hold the ball before the delivery—one second, two seconds or three seconds. Dancing off the base, he counted the seconds, and usually he took off at the split-second the pitcher had committed himself to throw to the plate.

His record-breaking 97th steal in 1962 tells something of his craftiness. "There I was," he once said in his hushed, dramatic way. He got up from a hotel-room chair and edged along the floor, arms extended, as though he were leading off base. "Everyone knew I was going to steal. I'd stolen 96. This one would break Ty Cobb's record. The pitcher, the catcher, they all knew I was going. It didn't seem I had a chance.

"Then it came to me"—he snapped his fingers—"a delayed steal. The pitcher throws, the catcher sees me not moving, and relaxes. *Bang!* I take off. The catcher says, 'Oh, gee, there he goes.' He hurries his throw, the ball bounces in the dirt, and I slide in head first. I'm safe. I've got my 97th steal. I've got the record."

Maury was 5-foot-10, 165 pounds during most of his career, with rippling muscles on his arms and legs and a weightlifter's hard chest. But he looked smaller. His Dodger teammates called him Mousy. As a child he'd been small, and though he was always strong, a hard-throwing pitcher in high school, his size did not impress scouts. Wills was born on October 2, 1932, in Washington, D.C., one of 13 children of an impoverished minister. In spite of his size, he excelled in basketball and football, using his speed and quickness to flit around bigger men.

When he was 16, a pitcher on the Cardozo High School baseball team, he went to a tryout camp attended by big league scouts. In two innings he struck out six batters, but he got no offers from the scouts. "They couldn't believe a little guy could throw a ball that fast," Wills once said, grinning.

In 1951 a Dodger scout did sign him for a small bonus. Because they thought him

Sliding into third base in a cloud of dust, Wills chalks up his 104th stolen base of 1962. The throw from the catcher got away from Giant third baseman Jim Davenport and Wills scored on the play.

too small to be a pitcher, the Dodgers converted him into an infielder. From 1951 to 1958 he scratched around the minors, nearly always hitting between .270 and .300, but the Dodger organization thought he was too small ever to be a big league hitter.

Wills began to think so, too. "I was a baseball bum," he once said of his eight years in the minor leagues. "I was content to bounce around, not learning much, not caring much. I was sure I'd never get out of the minors."

There were two turning points in his career. The first came in 1958 when he was playing for Spokane. His manager, Bobby Bragan, taught him to hit lefthanded so he could be a switch-hitter. It was the first big challenge he'd ever faced up to as a ballplayer. As he developed into a good lefthanded hitter, he gradually realized that baseball was an art to be worked at and mastered.

Late in the 1959 season, scrapping with the Braves and Giants for a pennant, the Dodgers needed a shortstop and called up Maury. He hit .260 and made several glittering plays in the field. The Dodgers won the pennant and the World Series.

Early in the 1960 season, though, he was batting only .208. Manager Walter Alston dropped him to eighth spot in the lineup and frequently took him out for a pinch hitter late in the game when the Dodgers were losing. In one game Alston took him out in the third inning.

Wills felt humiliated. He sought out Dodger coach Pete Reiser for advice on being a better hitter. Working with Maury three hours a day before games, Reiser taught him how to look for the pitch he should hit. Most important, he instilled in Maury the confidence that he could be a better hitter.

In one game Maury went four for four

against Philadelphia. His average began to climb. He lifted it nearly a hundred points, finishing the season at .295. In almost every season after that, Wills batted above .275.

The Dodgers traded Wills to the Pirates in 1966 but he returned to Los Angeles in 1969. To baseball fans of the 1960s, he symbolized those smart defensive Dodger teams of the 1960s that won pennants in 1963, 1965 and 1966. The Dodgers had no home run hitter and little batting strength. But they had two overpowering pitchers, Sandy Koufax and Don Drysdale, and a tight defense, plus the base-stealing Maury Wills. Usually they beat opponents with scores of 1–0, 2–1, or 3–2.

A typical Dodger victory came against Houston in 1962. With the score tied 3–3 in the 14th inning, Wills got a walk. He stole second, then stole third. He flew home to score on a fly to shallow right field, sliding in ahead of the throw, and the Dodgers won, 4–3.

The American League was stung by Maury's base-running daring in a 1962 All-Star game. In the eighth inning of a 1–1 game, Maury led off with a single. When Jim Davenport singled to left, Wills rounded second base and took a wide turn, feinting toward third. The American League's left-fielder, Rocky Colavito, picked up the ball and cocked it, challenging Maury to dare to go to third.

Maury jigged between second and third. Colavito, proud of his strong arm, threw the ball on a line to second base, planning to fool Maury by throwing behind him and catching him in a rundown. But Maury took off for third base. He slid in, head-first, ahead of the throw from second and moments later he scored on a fly ball. The National League won the game, 3–1.

Maury Wills' flying feet had helped to win another ball game.

LARRY WILSON

Larry Wilson, defensive safety for the St. Louis football Cardinals, waited anxiously as the New York Giant quarterback Charley Conerly began calling signals. Wilson was standing at his usual spot, six yards from the line of scrimmage. At the snap of the ball Wilson burst straight ahead. No one stopped him and he brought Conerly down before Conerly knew what had happened.

"I'll never forget the look on Conerly's face," Wilson said later. "His eyes popped out to here."

Conerly had a right to be surprised. He had been playing football over 20 years, but he had never seen a safety shoot in on him like that. Normally safeties always stayed in the backfield to protect against the pass or run.

Wilson used this technique—called the safety blitz—for the first time against the Giants in that 1961 game. It remained his specialty through the rest of the decade. Other defensive backs tried to copy him, but no one did it with quite the same dangerous flair.

The success of the safety blitz hinged on

Larry Wilson (8) grabs Philadelphia running back Harry Jones during a 1967 game.

surprise. If the opponent knew it was coming, the 6-foot, 190-pound Wilson was in trouble. In a 1962 game against Pittsburgh, two big Steeler blockers were ready for Wilson. They both hit him, nearly knocking Wilson out. Larry later said he came out of the play faster than he went in. But twice in the same game Wilson got to quarterback Bobby Layne, knocking him for losses before Layne could even raise his arm to throw the ball.

"Larry Wilson should be 93 years old after all the tackles he's made," Layne said in admiration. "Larry Wilson is the toughest guy in football."

Toughness is something Larry Wilson has had all his life. He was born on March 24, 1938, in Rigby, Idaho, a town of about 1,000 people. When he was ten his mother died of spinal meningitis. Larry's father never remarried, raising his two sons by himself. One thing their father impressed on them was toughness. "Out in our country you've got to have guts," his father said. "If you don't have any, you're a nobody."

At Rigby High School, Larry starred in football, basketball, baseball and track. He wanted to go to college at Idaho State, but his father persuaded him to go to the University of Utah, which had a major-college football program. Larry was glad he listened. "If I hadn't gone to Utah," he said years later, "I might never have played pro ball."

Larry was a running back at Utah, playing one season for coach Jack Curtice and two for coach Ray Nagel. "With Coach Curtice," Larry said, "I learned the fun of the game. With Coach Nagel I learned how important it is to out-hit the other team."

In his senior year, Wilson led the team in scoring with 84 points, averaged 5.7 yards a carry and caught 21 passes. He was selected to no All-America teams but the Cardinals picked him in the seventh round of the professional football draft.

In his first test with the Cardinals he was a dismal failure. He played cornerback against the Baltimore Colts in a preseason game. His assignment was to cover All-Pro pass receiver Raymond Berry. Berry ran two pass patterns against Wilson. On the first one he scored on a 40-yard pass play and on the second he got to the one-yard line.

When Larry got back to the sideline he felt crushed. "I never want to play this game again," he told another player.

For the next three exhibition games Larry sat on the bench. He expected to be cut from the squad before the regular season began. But in the last preseason game he got a break. Because of an injury to another player he was sent in at safety, a position he had never played before. But safety turned out to be his natural position. That day he kept San Francisco's R. C. Owens from catching a single pass. Within weeks Larry Wilson was a regular.

The safety blitz soon became Larry's most spectacular claim to fame, but it wasn't his only one. Wilson had an uncanny ability to anticipate a pass pattern and beat the receiver to the ball. Once he made seven interceptions in seven games, and he was among the league leaders in interceptions every year.

Wilson also tackled like a man fifty pounds heavier. "When he tackles you, you know it," said end Pete Retzlaff of the Philadelphia Eagles. "He hits as hard as anybody in the league."

In the summer of 1965, Pittsburgh Steeler coach Buddy Parker was watching a film of an exhibition game between St. Louis and San Francisco. Parker was supposed to be scouting the 49ers, since they were his next opponent. But he couldn't take his eyes off

Wilson. "Get me a pair of scissors," he finally said to an assistant.

Parker snipped out Wilson's plays, spliced them together into a separate film and showed it to his players the next day. When the film was over, Parker flipped on the lights. He looked around at his team and said, "If all you men would only play football half as well as Larry Wilson, we'd win every game."

Later that season Wilson put on his most unforgettable display of courage and skill. In the first half of a game against the Giants he landed on the middle finger of his right hand while making a tackle. The finger bothered him and he knew something was wrong. The trainer taped the finger at halftime. Then, in the second half, his left hand got jammed in a pileup. The pain increased as the day wore on. After the game X-rays

A safety's big job is pass defense. Here Wilson takes a pass out of the hands of Cleveland receiver Gary Collins.

Waiting to get back into play, Wilson watches the Cardinal offensive unit.

showed that Wilson had broken a bone across the back of his left hand and had fractured a finger on his right hand.

The doctor put both of Larry's hands in casts. But that didn't stop Larry. He practiced all week, even though he couldn't cut his food or button his shirt. On the day of the game the trainer put foam rubber pads over the casts and wrapped them in adhesive tape. "You look like a boxer," the trainer said, laughing.

Larry laughed too, and then went out and made one of the big plays of the day. He intercepted a Pittsburgh pass with his "boxing gloves" and ran it back 34 yards. This set up a touchdown, which helped the Cardinals win, 21–17.

Wilson played the next week, too, but when the doctor examined Larry's hands after the game, he discovered that the bro-

ken finger on the right hand was sliding down. "Your finger is shorter now," said the doctor. "The more you play, the worse it will get. I can't let you play anymore. You need surgery."

Larry gave in and missed the next four games. He returned for the last game of the season, against Cleveland. With his hands still protected by the foam rubber, he intercepted three passes. He ran one of them back 96 yards for a touchdown.

The seasons rolled by and Larry proved to be as steady a performer as any in pro football in the 60s. He seldom had a bad game, or a bad season. He received many game balls, which are awarded by a winning team to its outstanding player. He was named each year as a safety on the All-Pro team. And his courage made him one of the most popular players in the game.

CARL YASTRZEMSKI

In the late fall of 1958, the Boston Red Sox signed Carl Yastrzemski for one of the largest bonuses in their history. They paid $100,000 to the 19-year-old slugger. Of course they expected a lot in return. They knew that the great Ted Williams would be playing only a year or two more, and they considered Yaz his replacement as a star hitter.

For his first pro season Yaz was sent to Raleigh of the Class B Carolina League. He got off to a slow start, but by the end of the year he had won the batting championship with a .377 average. Once the Raleigh season had ended, in early September, the Red Sox brought him to Boston to work out before a game. The lefthanded-hitting Yaz amazed everyone when he drove two pitches into the distant right field bullpen.

Yaz spent the rest of September with Minneapolis of the Triple-A American Association. In the spring of 1960, at the Red Sox training camp, Yaz earned Ted Williams' personal stamp of approval. "Don't ever change, kid," Ted told him, "or let anyone try to change your batting style. It's perfect."

The Red Sox sent Yaz to Minneapolis for the 1960 season. Just as at Raleigh, Yaz got off to a slow start. But again he came on strong as he got to know the pitchers. By August he was hitting .310. Anyone else would have been thrilled with that average, but Yaz wasn't. He still trailed the league-leading hitter, Larry Osborne, by 35 points.

"I'll catch him," he told a friend one day.

"Relax, forget it. You can't catch Osborne with three weeks left," the friend said. "Do you expect to lead every league you play for in hitting?"

"Yes," said Yaz, matter-of-factly.

Then he went out and began proving how serious he was. He got at least one hit a game for 30 straight games, and with two games left in the season he was ahead of Osborne. On the last two days Carl had 4 hits in 9 at-bats, which normally would have been more than enough to clinch the batting title. But Osborne had an even better two days, going 8-for-10, and finally beating out Yaz for the title, .342 to .339. Yaz had to be satisfied with a trophy as the top rookie of the league.

Yastrzemski's sizzling finish and his great self-confidence told the Red Sox all they needed to know about him. They brought him up to the majors. Within three years Yaz was living up to not only the Red Sox' expectations, but his own. He won the American League batting title in 1963 with a .321 average. Four years later he won it again, and he captured it a third time in 1968.

It was the second title, in 1967, that meant the most to Yaz and the Red Sox. Boston began the season as a 100–1 shot to win the pennant but were swept along by Yaz's clutch hitting and fielding. By the end of the year Yaz had won the Triple Crown with a .326 average, 44 home runs, and 121 runs batted in. Yaz was a near-unanimous choice for Most Valuable Player, and Boston won its first pennant since 1946.

All of New England was delirious over Yaz and the Red Sox that year. But happiest of all was a Polish-American potato farmer in Bridgehampton, New York, who stayed close to his radio and TV when he couldn't get to Boston for the games. His name was Carl Yastrzemski, Sr., and he had put a lot of effort into turning Carl Jr. into a ballplayer.

Carl Jr. was born in nearby Southampton on the shores of Long Island on August 22, 1939. When he was old enough, he began helping with the work in the potato fields. And when the work was done, he and his dad would play ball. A Little League team was formed in town when Carl was 12 and it went on to win the Long Island championship. Carl switched between pitcher and shortstop. By the time he was 16 he was playing in a semi-pro league with his father and was already attracting major-league scouts. Bots Nekola, a scout for the Red Sox, sent a note to Boston raving about Yaz's perfect, level swing.

In his four years at Bridgehampton High School, Yaz hit over .500, and he pitched a no-hitter and a two-hitter in his last two games. He also was a great basketball player, breaking the Long Island scoring record as a senior with 628 points in 22 games.

By graduation, in 1957, Carl had 14 offers from major-league teams. But he turned them down to enter Notre Dame University. The following summer he again played semi-pro ball. He was now the regular shortstop, replacing his father who had switched to third. Carl Jr. was able to move around better, but his father, at 41, could still show him a thing or two about hitting. While Carl Jr. hit a respectable .345 that summer, Carl Sr. was hitting an incredible .455. When Bots Nekola sent a new report to the Red Sox, still raving about Carl Jr., the Boston farm director wrote Nekola back, saying, "I wonder if we're going after the wrong Yastrzemski."

Boston star Carl Yastrzemski follows through on his swing (top), and then heads for first (left) during the 1967 World Series against St. Louis.

Yaz returned to Notre Dame that fall but finally signed with the Red Sox during Thanksgiving vacation. He was used mainly as a second-baseman at Raleigh, and then was switched to the outfield for good at Minneapolis.

Ted Williams retired after the 1960 season and Red Sox manager Mike Higgins immediately announced that 21-year-old Carl Yastrzemski would be the replacement. The pressure on Yaz was tremendous and he did have his problems early in '61. "From the opening game the pitchers worked me over like I'd never been worked over before," Carl told a writer. "I became a pushover for a lot of them."

But he refused to be a pushover for long, and he didn't panic. He took many hours of extra batting practice, working his hands raw. And it paid off. In the last six weeks of the season he hit .350, to bring his final average up to .266. The next year it shot up to .296 and Yaz was the only man on the team to play every game.

In 1963 Yaz arrived as a full-fledged major league star. Besides winning the batting title, he led the league in hits and doubles. He was doing a fine job of replacing Williams, although his batting style reminded people more of Stan Musial, the St. Louis Cardinal Hall of Famer. Like Musial, Yaz held the bat high, and took an orthodox coiled stance.

Yaz was also colorful in the field. There was a touch of Willie Mays in him in the way he would charge a hit and then gun the ball to second. Often his aggressiveness kept a runner from taking an extra base.

In 1964, though, Yaz had a problem. He had been in big demand as a banquet speaker during the winter and had added 20 pounds to his normal 180-pound, 5–11 frame. He never could get in proper condition during the year, and his batting average dipped to .289. It would have been a good year for most players, but the fans had come to expect more than that from Ted Williams' successor.

Yaz was determined to redeem himself in '65. Every night that winter he went to the cellar and exercised. "I did everything from isometrics to just plain pushups," he said. "I could feel myself getting stronger and stronger. By February, I could hardly wait for training to start."

Three different times during 1965 Yaz had to come out of the lineup because of injuries, but even that couldn't stop him. He wound up hitting .312, second only to Minnesota's Tony Oliva.

The next season Yaz had his worst season ever, his average dropping to .278. People began to wonder if Yaz was only going to tease them with greatness and never quite achieve it.

Yaz himself had always felt he would never reach his peak until the Red Sox were in a pennant race. He got his chance to prove his point in 1967, much to the surprise of everyone. The Red Sox were expected to be a second-division ball club, but they stayed near the front all season long. And they stayed there because of Yaz. "He has probably meant 30 victories to us," manager Dick Williams said during the last week of the season. "Maybe 20 games with his bat and another ten with his arm."

Going into the season's last two days, the Red Sox needed a bit of a miracle to win the pennant. They were host to Minnesota for a two-game series and trailed the Twins by one game. Meanwhile, Detroit had two doubleheaders coming up against California and they too trailed Minnesota by a game. So the Red Sox had to win both their games and the Tigers had to lose twice.

In the first game against the Twins, Yaz hit a three-run home run and the Red Sox

won, 6–4. The next day, with the Sox trailing, 2–0, and the bases loaded, Yaz lined a single to center to tie the score. Later, he also threw out a runner at second to end a Minnesota rally. The Red Sox won the game, 5–3. Three and a half hours later Detroit had lost its second game of the weekend and the Red Sox were American League champs.

On that final weekend Yaz hit 7-for-8, but his clutch performance went even beyond that. In the final 12 games he had hit .523, driven in 16 runs, scored 14 runs and hit five homers. His season's total of 44 home runs was more than twice what he'd ever hit before and it broke Ted Williams' team record. Yaz also went over 100 runs-batted-in for the first time. He was easily the league's Most Valuable Player, and the only surprise in the voting was that one baseball writer voted for someone else.

In the World Series against the Cardinals, Yaz continued as the Red Sox hero. In the first game he starred defensively. On one play he made a backhand catch of a line drive near the left field wall; on another he threw out Julian Javier at the plate. But the Red Sox lost, 2–1, and Carl was upset that he went 0-for-4 against Bob Gibson at the plate. He even went out after the park had been cleared and took extra batting practice. No one could ever remember that being done at a World Series before.

The next day Yastrzemski came up in the fourth inning with a man on. Dick Hughes threw him a high inside fast ball and Yaz hit it into the right field stands. In the seventh inning two men were on when Yaz came up. He hit another home run, farther than the first. "Right now," he said afterward, "home runs seem as easy as singles used to."

The Red Sox won the second game, 5–0, to tie the Series, but the Cardinals went on to win it all in seven games. As for Yaz, there was little more he could have done. He hit .400 and got a third home run. After the Series, when Fenway Park had to be made ready for the Boston Patriots football team, Yaz took home some of the sod in left field as a memento of his and the Red Sox' great season.

There was no pennant for the Red Sox in '68, but there was at least some personal satisfaction for Yaz with his third batting title. He hit .301 in a year dominated by great pitching. He was the only hitter in the league to break .300. The next season Yaz's average dropped to an all-time low of .255, but he became a slugger again with 40 home runs and 111 runs-batted-in.

By the end of the decade he had given Red Sox fans nine exciting years. They were not all great ones to be sure, because Yaz was subject to the ups and downs of most human beings. But his overall value to the Red Sox was more than recognized by owner Tom Yawkey. Yaz received a $140,-000 contract for the 1970 season, making him baseball's highest paid player. And he was still only 30 years old, giving him a chance of being a star through the 1970s.

Yastrzemski makes a leaping backhand catch of Curt Flood's line drive in the fifth inning of the first game of the 1967 World Series. The Red Sox lost the Series in seven games.

INDEX

Page numbers in italics refer to photographs